D0646110

sex talk

Uncensored Exercises

for Exploring

What Really Turns You On

Aline P. Zoldbrod, Ph.D.
Lauren Dockett

New Harbinger Publications, Inc.

Publisher's Note

*This publication is designed to provide accurate and authoritative informa-
tion in regard to the subject matter covered. It is sold with the understanding
that the publisher is not engaged in rendering psychological, financial, legal,
or other professional services. If expert assistance or counseling is needed, the
services of a competent professional should be sought.*

Distributed in the U.S.A. by Publishers Group West; in Canada by Raincoast
Books; in Great Britain by Airlift Book Company, Ltd.; in South Africa by
Real Books, Ltd.; in Australia by Boobook; and in New Zealand by Tandem
Press.

Copyright © 2002 by Aline Zoldbrod and Lauren Dockett
       New Harbinger Publications, Inc.
       5674 Shattuck Avenue
       Oakland, CA 94609

Cover design by Amy Shoup
Cover photos by Jon Feingersh/Corbis/Stock Market Photo (above) and
 White Packert/Image Bank/Getty Images (below)
Edited by Wendy Millstine
Interior design by Michele Waters

ISBN 1-57224-286-8 Paperback

All Rights Reserved

Printed in the United States of America

New Harbinger Publications' Web site address: www.newharbinger.com

04 03 02

10 9 8 7 6 5 4 3 2 1

First printing

To the memory of my brilliant, funny, and lusty friend, Carolyn.

—A.P.Z.

To Maria Tarbox Dea, who can always get me talking. With love,

—L.D.

Contents

Part II From Shy To Shock-Free
Banishing Guilt and Inhibition with Talk   35

Acknowledgments

Heaps of gratitude from the both of us to Wendy Millstine and Heather Garnos Mitchener, for sex positive editing with flair. Our thanks to all the creative geniuses at NH who had a hand in this, including Catharine Sutker, Amy Shoup, Kirk Johnson, Michele Waters, Tracy Powell, Lorna Garano, and Gretchen Gold.

Aline says: I would like, first and foremost, to thank Lauren Dockett, who conceived of this project and invited me to join. I am so pleased that I had the chance to work with her on this bicoastal enterprise. It makes me feel so "with it" to have written a book with someone who lives and works three thousand miles away. I had sworn that I would never try to write a book with another person. But I feel so simpatico with Lauren that I thought I'd try it. Batting ideas back and forth was a creative treat. The whole experience was seamless, remarkably fun, and exhilarating.

Truth be told, I could not have had this modern experience of writing a book with someone who lives three thousand miles away without the help of my husband, who did the fancy technical stuff for me. I'm just not that modern. So thank you, Larry.

Finally, I have to thank my family and friends, for their ongoing and consistent encouragement and support. And I thank my parents, both gone now, for teaching me that it is safe to love and trust and connect with others. I truly am blessed.

Lauren says: I would like to offer love and thanks to the brilliant, incomparably funny, and divinely soulful Aline Z.—it was every minute a pleasure. Thanks as always to my sister, folks, and family: this time for having a sense of humor about it all. And a final word to my community of friends who have passed through or are still in the San Francisco Bay Area, for the acceptance and encouragement of lives lived beyond the pale—you bring me joy.

Introducing . . .
SEX TALK

How would you feel if every unhealthy sexual inhibition you have suddenly disappeared? How about if a partner you'd thought had lost all desire for you unexpectedly turned to you after a surprising and steamy session of lovemaking and said, "Baby, that is the best time I have ever had"? Sound far-fetched? You'd think. But what if it's not? We all have the potential to be sexually free, to satisfy ourselves and our partners, and to reach pinnacles of sexual joy. Each of us has that potential, whatever our age or the status of our relationship. And the secret to realizing it is something we do every day of our lives. The secret is talk.

We're not just referring to dirty talk. Although we will, and it'll be fun. What we mean is no-holds-barred honest talk. Telling each other the truth in a heartfelt way about what it really takes for each of us to turn on, to roll over, and to howl is the ticket to a happy, healthy sex life.

Sound fun? Scary? Stay with us . . .

For some of us, talking about sex seems tantamount to taking a cold shower, and for others, like facing a firing squad. Isn't talk the antithesis of carnal fun? Terribly risky? Not if you know what we know. In reality, it's the *not talking* that keeps so many of us from having the sex that we want. It's the fear of appearing freaky, or hurting someone's feelings, or introducing something new into a tried and true mix, that dulls and ruins sex lives and relationships. Silence is the true enemy of sexual pleasure. Talk is its greatest ally.

Talk dissolves fears. It unearths desires. Talk builds trust and conspiratorial highs. Talk is sexy. The right talk can have you both giggling hysterically. It can start off with you red-faced and bumbling, and end in happy tears. It can result in a sexual feast, a non-physical glimpse at one another's souls, a plan for a titillating future, or a healing from a long-held pain.

But it's true, there are some wrong ways to talk. Ways that you can make your partner feel bad, or yourself defeated. We want you to learn the right ways. The fifty right ways to be exact, to break free from fear and into trust, to discover where your true pleasure really lies, to come together in ways that had stopped seeming possible, and to make the most of the love you have.

We've compiled simple and safe Sex Talk exercises that anyone can do. Regardless of your age, the length of your relationship, your sexuality, or your preferences, these fifty ways can be practiced in any order, some once, others over and over—whatever feels right to you. You can read this book on your own or over the breakfast table with your partner. So feel free to just open the book to any page and get going.

Enjoy! There's nothing like a good Sex Talk!

PART I

Getting It Clearly

Communication That Works

The Best Sex You Ever Had

Jamie and Sam stopped along the highway to fill up on gas and grab some snacks for the road. They found themselves side by side in the chip aisle of a small-town filling station, where the pickings were slim and Jamie's allergy to nuts was something of a problem.

"Ahhh," Sam said, bumping Jamie and grabbing hold of a bag of old-time chips. "I remember these."

On one of their first road trips Sam had fed Jamie the chips as she drove. He was careful at first, but then playfully stuffed whole fistfuls into Jamie's mouth, until Jamie was laughing and spitting them into her lap. When she went to brush them off her legs and onto the floor, Sam stopped her, bent over, and gathered them with his tongue. Soon they'd pulled to the side of the road, taken a blanket from the trunk, and were having glorious, trespassing sex among the tall grasses and cicadas of a southern afternoon.

"That," Sam said, as they stood grinning in line, "was some of the best sex we've ever had."

"It was nice," Jamie said.

"The little bit of danger, the smell of that ground, the way you looked with your hair in the grass, moaning into the sun," Sam said. "God, I still think about it a lot."

When they climbed back into the car, Jamie told Sam about her favorite memory. "I loved that time after we came back from your mother's. It was our first Sunday to ourselves and we couldn't keep our hands off each other. I wanted you so much that day. Every time we came it was just like a little buildup for the next time. We seemed to say and do everything we wanted. The ice, the tying up, that fantasy of yours. It was as if we knew how much we both wanted it and so there were no limits."

Our Best Talk

One of the ways to give and receive more of what you want sexually with one particular partner is to build on the high points of your own sexual history together. Flip through your memories and zero in on one time that really blew the others out of the water. What was it about that time? Where were you? What were you doing and for how long? How were the physical sensations different? Were they heightened? Prolonged? Did you feel electric? Did you take it slow? Hard and fast? Was your desire heightened before you got together, or did you do something that raised the temperature together? Do you remember how you were feeling emotionally at the time? Were you in love? Frustrated? Were you making up after a fight or trying to prevent one?

Tell each other what really worked that one time. And make plans to incorporate some of those elements into a new session. If it happened in a plane lavatory at thirty thousand feet, then imagine where you can recreate those sensations on the ground. Plan now. The best is a great place to start!

Loving Critiques

Gerald and Marie finish their lists and lay back on their lounge chairs. Marie reaches for Gerald's hand and slowly spins the band on his ring finger. It is a habit that Gerald is fond of and one that Marie has kept long these twenty-four years. Marie clears her throat and starts:

"Oral sex on me until I have an orgasm. Check! Willingness to pause during intercourse when my vagina becomes dry. Check! Able to tell when I've gotten dry with no prompting from me. Double-check! Really exceptional, sir!"

"Why thank you."

"Whispers sexy things to me before making love. Check! Whispers dirty things to me during sex. No check! Not bad so far, mister, but that last one gets a minus."

"Yes, fair enough. Even the best of us, you know."

"Okay, then there is this teeny issue of changing positions. You get a check because you are so very smooth in the way you move us around. It's very sexy."

"Really?"

"Yes, it makes me feel like I'm in very capable hands. I love it."

"Well, honey, you are very smooth yourself. In fact, you get a check on my list for 'likes to do it in interesting ways.'"

"Well you know I do! I really do. I was just thinking on that one, that sometimes those interesting ways get *really* interesting, and I think I'd like to keep at them for longer than we do."

"You mean I'm going too fast."

"Not always. I'm thinking of one time in particular. That last time we were in the Jacuzzi. Do you remember?"

"Of course I do!"

"Yes, that was really great. I was starting to be able to push back until I felt you might be on my G-spot."

"No!"

"It was getting there, I think."

"And I went and lost my footing!"

"No, it's fine, honey. That part was funny, and sweet really. I just wish we could have resumed. Maybe I just should have told you."

"Or I could have asked. I was flustered. But yes, tell me next time. And put a minus there next to your check and a little note that says 'Jacuzzi.' We will definitely try that one again."

Gentle Critic's List

What Gerald and Marie are engaged in is a list-making exercise that allows them to identify their sexual likes and to see whether these likes are being addressed within the relationship in ways that satisfy them. This exercise also allows them to gently introduce complaints. It is very important to remember that a flat-out critique of your partner's sexual abilities not only creates conflict in your relationship, it is also mean! We have heard so many people, when asked why they are afraid to open up to a new lover sexually, cite fears of disappointing this new lover in the same ways they'd been told they were disappointing to others. Many people are able to hear about their partner's desires for untried sexual techniques without taking offense. But when we're told NOT to do something that we have been doing, that's when our feelings can get hurt. Always express your sexual complaints in a gentle, loving fashion and with an awareness of how it may affect your partner. One of the gentlest ways is to incorporate those complaints into "the list."

First, write down your sexual likes. This will encourage the required clarity, thoughtfulness, and tact you'll need for discussion.

Next, go through your own list and place checks next to those likes that are being fulfilled and minus signs next to those that still need doing. Then gently discuss the modification that you're after with your partner. Make sure that your complaint is not the first thing you read to your partner. It is certainly your prerogative to have the kind of sex that you want, and to ask that your likes be fulfilled in the best way possible. But remember that it is a gift to have love and sex in your life. Give appreciation for this at the outset.

Knowing What We Want Before We Ask

Suzanne has started dating again three months after the end of her twenty-year relationship. The new woman she is seeing makes her weak in the knees. And Suzanne spies an openness in Lynn that she is hopeful will extend to the bedroom. Before she sleeps with her, however, Suzanne wants to be able to tell Lynn about her sexual likes and dislikes. In her old relationship, Jonathan was the more dominant lover. He and Suzanne set up a small repertoire of sexual acts from which they barely deviated. Suzanne knows that she wants a real smorgasbord of options this time, but isn't exactly sure about the various dishes. Even now, she moans to herself, now that she's a woman in her forties, she still doesn't know.

Focusing on Yourself

Before you get into new sexual situations, you should always do yourself the favor of thinking about what you want out of them. Even if you are in a long-term relationship and just want things to change, you need to be able to understand for yourself and be able to tell your lover what those "things" are. The best way to do this is to take some time alone to both discover your turn-ons and explore them by yourself.

Your ability to know what you currently want may depend a great deal on your own inhibitions. Are you willing to work through some of those to find out what you might really enjoy? Once you can say yes to this question, give yourself a chance to see and read about and taste and touch and feel a whole host of new sexual experiences.

1. *Masturbation.*

Mother Nature's own sexual learning tool is a sensational place to begin. Through masturbation you can find out exactly what kind of genital touches you find most exciting. Most men have had experience masturbating long before they have partnered sex. There is some speculation that this is because penises are difficult for boys to ignore. They pop out and call for attention, and they need to be held every time a guy pees. Often later in life, men discover that they have sensation in their nipples and in and around their anus.

However, women's genitals and their socialization are different. If you are a woman and have either never masturbated, or want to know the various ways that other women successfully report doing it, check out a copy of *The Hite Report* (1989). Remember that you needn't only learn how best to stimulate your clitoris. How does it feel to place something inside your vaginal walls? Which angles, pressures, and speeds of penetration work best? How do you like your breasts touched? Do you like the feel of something brushing past or pushing into your anus? Staff from the famed, women-friendly sex store Good Vibrations have lent their expertise to *The New Good Vibrations Guide to Sex* (Winks and Semons 1997) and *Good Vibrations: The New Complete Guide to Vibrators* (Blank and Whidden 2000) both of which offer useful ideas.

2. *Positions.*

New positions are a gas to study. How do some people stay in positions without falling over, tearing something, or passing out? For some eye-opening ideas about new positions, we recommend turning to the wisdom of the ages. Find a modern, illustrated edition of the two thousand-year-old Indian classic, the *Kama Sutra*. Then get some Post-its and flag anything that looks good. When the time comes, have a field day with your imagination and your partner.

You can also discover new positions by watching erotic movies and finding free erotic sites on the Internet. However, remember that the people in positions are paid to look like they're enjoying them. It may just make you feel dizzy to stand on your head while your partner gives you head!

3. *Sexual Fantasy.*

We have some favorite sources of sexual fantasy, which are books that include the real-life fantasies of both men and women. Famed women's issues and sex writer Nancy Friday has collected stories from people of all ages and sexes. We also recommend two books about fantasy from authors Iris and Steven Finz that are a hot read (see Resources). You can use fantasy secretly while in the midst of masturbation or sex, you can share particularly hot fantasies with your partner and use the language to fuel your sex, or you can make actual attempts to act them out.

4. *Imagery.*

Available personal imagery is a powerful way to discover what you want before you ask. Get ideas about what you like by "running a movie in your head" that contains the most wonderful encounters you've had with your partner or with other partners in your past. Be careful here if you are going to share this information. Comparing your current lover to your past lovers is a sure way of making him or her anxious. Instead of saying, "George had this sexy way of tickling the inside of my thigh with his erect penis, I was hoping you would do it too," try telling your partner that the idea of him putting his erect penis on your thigh and teasing you with it would be a turn-on.

Shopping for Sex

When Guy and Diane were first together, each surprised the other by bringing new and yummy sexual techniques to the relationship. Diane, for example, after reading a book about extending orgasms, had learned that grasping and gently pulling down on a man's testicles helped to both prolong his orgasm and add a new layer of pleasure to his experience. Guy, for his part, had seen an instructional porn film that showed women how to perform anal penetration on their partners. When he learned that Diane might be game, he bought the pinky-sized anal dildos that he had seen on the screen, a big bottle of lubricant, and slowly introduced them both to that end of the sexual spectrum!

Once aware of their partner's open-mindedness and interest in new sexual information, both Diane and Guy felt free to suggest repertoire-expanding searches. Now they like to read erotica and sex manuals aloud to each other, and to sample agreed-upon porn. Sometimes the stories and films jumpstart their sex, and at other times, offer them new inspiration. Just last week Diane blindfolded Guy, applied the sweet torture of a roaming ice cube to his erogenous zones, and rewarded him with a culminating taste of herself.

Sex Superstore

One of the first steps in understanding and expanding your sexual appetite, either on your own or in your relationship, is to give yourself a chance to see, read, taste, touch, and feel all kinds of sexual experiences. Whether you and/or you and your partner are both looking for new ideas, or you need help figuring out what really turns you on, take heart. There is a well-lit, open-all-hours sex superstore ready to fulfill your every need.

Let's start in the pornographic film aisle. If you want to begin watching porn together, many video stores (adult and otherwise) now have a "couples section" where they stock the videos that are billed female-friendly. If you are relying on the porn to make an evening for you, we suggest previewing at least part of it together at some other point, to make sure you are both interested in what you've rented. Also, if you'll be enjoying pornography on your own and don't know where to start, or if the idea of renting porn in public gives you hives, there are some online sites that will do the work for you. These sites view and rate films, and can tell you how to order them for discreet home delivery. Try the following companies, whose sites are listed in our Resources: Blowfish, Good Vibrations, and Toys in Babeland.

If you are interested in porn that has been made by and for women, we suggest anything by Femme Productions. Femme is a company headed by former porn star Candida Royalle, who does her own producing and directing. Some people find her work softcore, whereas others report it to be just right. See more information about Candida in our Resources section. Good Vibrations stocks and recommends a good selection of sex-positive, woman-friendly and gay, lesbian, and bisexual-friendly porn in their catalog, which is also available online (see Resources). If you want instructional videos that are also a turn-on, we suggest anything by sex experts and porn stars Nina Hartley and Annie Sprinkle, and the folks at Better Sex Videos (see Resources).

Many of our mothers and grandmothers knew the guilty pleasures of romance novels, which did a nice job of disproving the idea that women do not like to read or hear explicit stories of sex. These novels now share shelf space with mainstream but explicit erotica. There are too many tantalizing books of erotica to recommend, but if you can't find what you're looking for in your local bookstore, try Good Vibrations' sexuality library, the recommendations from the gals at Libida, or many of the online sources for sex store listings in our Resources. Also, if you are interested in reading short pieces of erotica online, try the Erotica Readers Association, Clean Sheets Magazine, or the Scarlet Letters Web sites (see Online Erotica Resources).

If you don't have a sex toy store where you live, or prefer to have the toy(s) arrive in a brown wrapper at your door, consult our list of trustworthy and sex positive sex toy dealers in the references section.

Some of what you see or find in the sex superstore may be wilder that anything you'll be doing yourself. But don't turn away from the wild images that have intrigued you. All the images and ideas that you let yourself discover are going to be very useful. Even if you decide on your own or with your partner that you don't want to try the hardcore new activity you've just read about, you can still bring this material into real life in the form of secret fantasies.

Happy shopping!

Laying Down the Ground Rules

Like many long-term couples, Alice and Dave experience fluctuations in their desire for sex. Alice has been pleasuring herself during the latest downturn and coming to terms with her persistent passivity in the sexual arena. Dave has asked her repeatedly over the years if she'd like to alter or expand their routine, and has complained about her inability to approach him for sex. Now that Alice is in her late thirties, her desire for sex seems to be on an upswing, but she is a little scared about suddenly transforming herself into a sex kitten.

What would happen if she started approaching Dave and he took that to mean that she now wanted it all the time? Or what if Dave started getting upset that she did want it? Maybe he would think she was turning slutty on him or suspect her of cheating.

Despite these fears, Alice can feel that the rise in her sexual desire is a good thing, and she can see how it could improve their relationship and offer real promise for their on-again, off-again sex life. But still, she needs to be sure that things aren't going to either get out of control or somehow backfire on her if she shares this with Dave.

Bonding Boundaries

No matter how far along you are in your relationship, if you've never established what you each do and don't want to happen in the sack, the time is nigh! We are not talking here about scripting every sexual encounter, rather we want you to lay out a few basic sexual ground rules that will free the both of you to be more comfortable and trusting in your roles as lovers.

For Alice, this might mean sitting down with Dave and telling him that she is ready to start asking for sex when she wants it. But she also needs to be sure that he won't respond to her at those moments like she is slutty, or assume that in general she has now become a sex bunny and be offended if she refuses his advances in the future.

For other couples, setting down ground rules comes out of understanding your turn-ons and turnoffs, knowing what has made you uncomfortable in the past, and sharing these with one another. Women especially are prone to be passive sexually, and allow their lovers to call all the shots. They can be in a much better position to get their dislikes honored and their needs and wishes met if they can successfully conceive of and establish a few sexual boundaries.

Take some time now to think about and discuss with your partner what you do and don't want out of the sexual interactions you will have in the near future. Remind each other not to be afraid of these rules and make an effort to both reassure each other that the ground rules will remain enforced for as long as necessary. There will still be plenty that you can do, and boundaries can even shift over time as people's appetites expand or change, and as trust levels deepen.

Red Light, Green Light

"Red, red, red, red," Jenna calls, and Maureen slows the dildo's thrusting to a stop.

She reaches her left hand out for the lube and looks down at Jenna for a decision. Jenna nods emphatically and Maureen laughs.

"You have some energy today, girl!"

Maureen slathers the dildo with lube, readjusts the straps that run along her hips, and enters Jenna slowly. Jenna grabs onto Maureen's hips and guides her deeper and deeper.

"Okay, green," she says, and Maureen starts to thrust, slowly at first, watching Jenna's face for signs of discomfort, then faster and faster until Jenna starts to match her and take on some of the effort.

They stay that way for minutes. Jenna is usually unable to come, but they still both love the way this feels. Maureen is just about to ask Jenna if she wants to roll over when Jenna puts a firm hand up on her stomach and says, "Okay, baby, red."

"Final red?" Maureen asks.

"Final red."

Maureen slides out of Jenna and unhooks the strap-on.

"That was good," Jenna says. "Burning though, there at the end."

"Want something different?"

"Yes," she says, rising to her knees. "Hand that thing over."

How to Ask for Sex to Stop Right in the Middle

Nearly everyone has difficulty being honest about asking for sex to stop when it hurts. Penises hurt if they are pulled too hard, and they can be permanently injured if they are bent at uncomfortable angles. Women who are aroused mentally but not able to become aroused physically often lack lubrication, so that the friction of penetration becomes painful. Also, the *tenting* of the vagina, which occurs during intense arousal, may not happen, so that a thrusting dildo or penis may hit a cervix.

It is important that you feel it is safe to ask the other person to stop the moment you feel any physical discomfort. But even when talking about pain, it helps to use humor. If you are shy, it might even be fun to make a game out of it. Remember the "red light/green light" game from childhood? Agree that if either of you is feeling pain, you can get the action to stop by yelling "red light." Of course, when the problem is solved, you can yell "green light" and get it on again.

Ideally, we'd like you to be able to tell your partner the moment any significant discomfort occurs. A good precursor to this is to confess any secrets about past painful episodes with your partner before you are in the middle of sex.

Person A, write down any past episodes in which you found sexual activity painful. Person B, do the same.

Now share your fears and the reasons you didn't talk about your physical discomfort before. How would you like the other person to change their behavior so that they do not hurt you? Take responsibility for your own actions or lack of action. What could you have done to make sure the pain did not occur? If the reason for the pain was any pattern that you assume will be repeated, plan ahead to address it. For instance, if a woman has a pattern of becoming dry during intercourse, it would be important to always keep a tube of lubricant nearby.

Body Maps

Walter and Nancy have new erogenous zones. Walter never knew that if Nancy pressed on the pad of skin between his scrotum and anus, he'd get a jolt of pleasure that would make him gasp. Now, it has gotten to the point where Nancy massages that part of him whenever her hands or mouth are on his penis, and it is driving him wild.

Nancy has discovered that having each of her toes thoroughly sucked can feel like a drawing out of that incredible moment before orgasm, and make her literally squirm in ticklish ecstasy. Walter loves kneeling before Nancy, resting her ankles on his chest, and watching the turn-on in her face as he slowly sucks every one of her ten toes.

Nancy and Walter are sixty-two and sixty-one respectively. They've been together for thirty-nine years. An old friend of Nancy's told her last month that her own husband was going down on her for the first time because she was finally ready to let him. She'd had no idea what she'd been missing all these years.

Sharing Body Maps

Our bodies and our sex lives are renewable resources. Sensitivities and willingnesses change over time. If we stay ever open to exploring these resources, we'll continue to discover new sexual treasures and territories.

Despite what each of us may think we know about our own and each other's erogenous zones, the truth is, if we haven't checked lately, we might be overlooking some pretty promising stuff. To find out where, and how, your partner especially likes being touched, stroked, kissed, licked, and pinched, first pick up those pencils. It's time to draw a body map.

Each of you draw an outline of your body, front and back. Artistic skills are not required; just make an outline like a gingerbread cookie. Get together your coloring supplies: green, yellow, and red crayons for both of you. Color in the map according to how much you like to be touched in all of the areas of your body. The color code is:

Green: I love to be touched here.

Yellow: Sometimes I like to be touched here; ask me.

Red: I don't like to be touched here.

Color your body map both front and back and trade maps with your partner. Talk about what you've learned that's new and promise to pay attention to each other's maps the next time you're sexual. Paying attention means really exploring those green areas, and after checking, also visiting the yellow. Remember that even the best maps need eventual updating. Keep those crayons in a trusty place.

Scents and Sexability

Ever since his return from a two-month trail assignment in the Andes, Jean's biologist partner has developed an aversion to regular bathing. The first time they had sex after his return, Jean tried her best to breathe through her mouth. Although this made her a little light-headed, she had some success with it until she found herself attempting his favorite tongue pressure on his particularly pungent balls. Jean was eventually able to pull him into the bath when they were done. That particular bath seemed to him to be a natural extension of their sex play. However, since then, he has steadfastly expressed his new commitment to "allowing our real tastes and smells" to fester.

Jean's partner's choice to shower just once a week is having a deleterious effect on their sex life. He's decided that a little bit of grunge is a righteous turn-on. Primitively sexy, he likes to say. Whereas for Jean, the only way she will now consider getting down and dirty with him is if he gets good and clean!

Natural Scents Exercise

You can get closer as a couple by honestly sharing your experiences—good and bad—with smelling each other. Commonly, a partner will withhold negative thoughts about a partner's odor (bad breath, perspiration, poor hygiene, vaginal or scrotum odor) in order to not hurt the other person's feelings. Of course, we encourage kindness in any kind of sensitive revelation. However, not telling the truth about how you feel about scent easily backfires. An expectation of a disagreeable odor can easily become so entrenched that one partner may permanently avoid a particular sexual situation, or specific act.

Our sense of smell is very powerful. Memories, information, and personal associations are all more directly tied to smell than to any of our other senses. So it is important to pay attention to your own and your partner's experiences of scent.

The goal of this exercise is to honestly share your positive and negative experiences of your partner's natural scent under different conditions.

List your positive experiences:

List your negative experiences:

List the changes you would like the other person to make in their behavior involving scent:

If it turns out that you both prefer a fairly clean partner, often times, a before-sex ritual of a shower or other ablution can wipe out most bad scent associations. Other couples report that flavored oils, syrups, even a stick of incense burning nearby, can also do the trick.

Whatever you choose, remember to continue to share your feelings honestly and kindly about your partner's personal scents.

Sex Before You

Jacob and Mira were in the third hour of their hike. They'd reached their halfway point, a still pond inhabited by a wayward flock of Canadian geese, and were headed back to the car. Jacob's knee had been acting up for the better part of an hour, and Mira was attempting to distract him from the pain with a steady stream of banter. After exhausting their descriptions of primary school teachers, Mira and Jacob decided they needed something truly compelling to discuss if they were to overpower the throbbing in his knee. It would have to be sex.

Now, Jacob and Mira are going into their second year together and have consciously attempted to minimize talk about their sexual histories. They've each been around the block and they know how these kinds of conversations can go. Someone always ends up feeling inadequate. There's the way the revelations go on to haunt one or both partners. There's also the way these talks seem to minimize what they have as a couple by putting it in the context of other affairs. And yet, withholding some significant past sexual experiences, by substituting small talk, feels a little strange.

"All right," Mira says. "I am going to tell you one true thing about my sexual past, and two made-up stories."

"What are the made-up stories for?"

"They are so you can guess for yourself what I've really done, and also so I can tell how much you might be able to handle."

"Fair enough."

"Okay. When I was, uh, fourteen, Jenny McGuire and I found her dad's girlie magazines and then spent the afternoon acting out everything we could."

"Whoa. Just the lesbian stuff?"

"No, everything. There were implements involved."

"Very industrious of you."

"Thanks."

"Okay, that's one. What else?"

"One of my exes had this obsession with trying to fist me. She had fairly small hands but big knuckles. Finally one day, after lots of help from her vibrator and copious amounts of lube, she succeeded."

"Did she move it around at all?"

"Uh, no, we just kind of held our breath for a minute. Then I told her I felt like I was going to pee, and she pulled it out."

"Hmm."

"Hmm, what?"

"Seems a little anticlimactic."

"Yeah, it was sort of like trying to get up the guts to do something for a long time, like hop on a scary ride, and then finally doing it, losing the thrill, and deciding once was enough."

"Other people seem to like it."

"Yeah, that's what I hear."

"Okay, so what's the third thing?"

"The third thing is . . . Let's see. Remember that guy I told you about from the crabshack? The one with the old Pinto and the obsession with Molly Hatchett."

"Oh no."

"Yes. In the back, by the pay phone."

"How far?"

"Third base."

"I'll have to remember that. Play you some hard rock to get you in the mood."

"It might only work if you have a Pinto."

"Good to know."

"So, what do you think?"

"The fisting."

"What? How did you know?"

"I was just guessing really. But the pee detail smacked of experience."

"You're good."

Two Hypotheticals and a Truth Exercise

It's hard to take the risk of sharing your personal history, no matter how long you've been together. Some couples get it over with in the beginning. Others don't talk about it at all. But many people are much too curious to let these questions about their partner's past go unasked. Some of us have been very, very good, while others have been enviably bad! Some of us are in-between. How do we get the data about each other's past sexual experiences in a way that not only isn't threatening but is also fun? How do you figure out whether telling the truth about who you are and where you've been sexually will scare off the person?

We suggest the "two hypotheticals and a truth" exercise. Take a few minutes to think about some of the things about your sexual past that you're scared to share. One example might be that you're a virgin. Another might be that you've had two hundred sexual partners. Whatever the data is that you're scared to share, do it in the "two lies and a truth" format and take it slowly.

Group each of your "scary" facts with two other surprising, but utterly untrue, stories. Present your partner with the three items together and have them try to guess which one is the true fact, and which are lies.

Good to Hear

Sandra is ready for a change. For the last six months or more, she and George have been having the same sex. Same start, same quick progression from kissing to oral sex to intercourse, same not-so-big finish. It's not that the sex is bad exactly. George is still careful to attend to Sandra, and he has become very competent at stimulating her clitorally during intercourse—something they're both rather proud of. But the new predictability they're facing is unsatisfying enough to warrant Sandra's attention.

Sandra and George have been down this road before. Eighteen years of togetherness and they're bound to know the road fairly well. Before she introduces the problem, Sandra wants George to remember that she values his skills as a lover and that she loves much of what they do together in bed. She snuggles up to him on the couch and starts there.

"Hi."

"Hi."

"You're cute."

"Who, me?"

"Stunning really."

"I don't know about that."

"I love the way you look. At Tom's party last weekend you were so striking in the midst of all those sad other men."

"Naw."

"Yeah, really. Plus you smelled so yummy. You always smell yummy."

"I do?"

"Right here, on your neck, under your hairline, like tropical fruit."

"That tickles."

"You look good, you smell good, you taste good. And you are a pro in the sack."

"Are you trying to seduce me, flatterer?"

"I'm just trying to make the point that you are devastatingly attractive and a fabulous lover."

"Can we record this?"

"I think, the next time we have sex, we should linger some more on how beautiful your body is and how good you taste. Turn it into a sensual feast."

"A feast?"

"Yes. A slow, delicious feast."

"God that sounds good."

"That way I can also linger in your touch. How good I feel when you're licking my breasts. How amazing it is to watch your face when you are inside me. You know, I see you like that throughout my day. I flash on your face, and the muscles in your shoulders when you're holding yourself up."

"You do?"

"Yep."

"When you're on the train?"

"No, at work. When I'm on the train I can close my eyes. And then I think about the whole shebang. About kissing you and your tongue in my ear and how your ass feels in my hands when we're fucking."

"Jesus, honey."

"What do you think about the feast idea?"

"I think there's nothing on this stupid television anyway."

Purely Complimentary Talk

This is the place to assess the things your partner does sexually that you like very much. This list is important because your partner will not feel safe with you, or close to you, if you make him/her feel incompetent sexually. So before you ask for changes, it is important to give credit for what is going well sexually in these very concrete ways:

Things I like about my partner's looks:

Things I like that my partner does:

Things I like about my partner's smell:

Things I like about my partner's taste:

Things I love that we do together:

Think of this as the heaping spoon full of sugar you're giving before the medicine. It makes everything go down easier!

PART II

From Shy to Shock-Free

Banishing Guilt and Inhibition with Talk

Fear Schmear

Joey and Pamela are reuniting after a two-year separation from their fourteen-year relationship. Pamela is ready for Joey to begin coming home with her and spending the night. She is especially ready after their warm, hand-holding dates, and the heated make-out sessions in her driveway. But every time she places her hand solidly on Joey's crotch and invites him out of the steamed-up front seat and into the house, he says no. Instead, Joey runs his fingers through her hair and explains that he wants to savor this time, to wait until he feels they're both "really ready." Unfortunately, Joey isn't able to tell Pamela when that might be, and privately confesses that the idea scares him so much, he'd like to postpone it indefinitely. Now, Joey's hesitation would be perfectly acceptable, even commendable, if it was fueled only by respect for their new connection. But both of them are becoming concerned that waiting a long time to be sexual again is more indicative of a problem than it is Joey's care around their new togetherness.

Joey, when pressed, has admitted that as their relationship was coming apart, he had his first experiences of impotence. The impotence was devastating for him and he and Pamela were fighting so much at the time, she was never in the right frame of mind to be supportive and help him through it. Joey is also afraid that Pamela might have been with other men in the intervening years and that his old lovemaking style will now pale in comparison.

What Scares You

Even if we aren't in the delicate space of trying to negotiate a reunion with our partners, many of us, no matter how long we've been in our relationship, continue to be plagued by fears of our own inadequacies, or haunted by some kind of sexual dysfunction. Now we know that sexual freedom is about understanding and expressing and getting what you want sexually, but, just as importantly, it is also about being able to admit what scares you.

All of us have fears about being sexual. Some of us are afraid that we don't know how to "do it" right. Some of us are afraid we have done it "too much" or "too little" or with the wrong people. Some of us are afraid that because of some dysfunction, we can't "do it" right, no matter how hard we try. Most of the time, the fears boil down to concerns about being rejected by someone we love or want to stay close with. But the magic of being sexual with a person you trust is that it doesn't have to be perfect. That's part of the point of it. At its best sex is free, spontaneous, and playful. That's it.

1. Make a mental list of all of your sexual worries. Try to imagine that your partner has those very same worries. Now imagine a dialogue with your partner, where you reassure him or her that you don't expect perfection. Once you can create an imaginary acceptance from your partner, it will be easier to calm your own fears.

2. Approach your partner about this exercise. If they feel comfortable, ask them to also make a mental list and understand that you will respond gently to this

list. Once you've both established that you want to hear one another's fears, write your lists out and read them to each other. Explore with each other any questions that arise. It is important to clarify the fears if necessary so that you are each fully understood. The next time the fear arises, you and your partner will be better able to identify and quiet it, and treat each other like the lovable, imperfect creatures you both are.

Disinhibition Coach

Judy has been talking to her friend Lynnette about how inhibited she's feeling now that Roger has come home. He had been overseas for months and she'd missed him like crazy this time. She had even fantasized about all the lewd and wonderful things she would do to him upon his return. But now that he's back, she feels like her same old inhibited self again. Shy. Unsure of his desires. Afraid that what she has to offer sexually cannot be enough to satisfy this worldly and attractive partner of hers.

The last time she got this way Lynnette dragged her to a bar, stuck a drink in her hand, and asked every man that came their way whether he thought Judy was hot enough to make a man happy. Judy was mortified, at first. But a couple of men went beyond the initial shouts of "Hell yes!" and sat down to get her story. When they heard her fears they assured her that she truly was sexy and also that her interest in sex with Roger and her willingness to try new things was not only all the sophistication she needed, but more than enough of an offer for any good man.

That next day Lynnette had brought Judy her old, beaten up copy of *The Joy of Sex* and brainstormed some seduction scenarios. She patted Judy's bottom when she left and turned from the lawn to shout "Go to town, my vixen friend!" loud enough to set the neighbor's dog barking.

A Coach of Your Own

Sometimes there are people in our lives who, through their unconventional daring, move us to look anew at the many ways of being in this world. They help us to understand how we might be brave and creative, and though their behavior may sometimes make us wince in polite company, secretly we're thrilled that they go around rocking so many boats.

These, dear readers, are just the kind of people you need with you in the bedroom!

Now, when we suggest that you find your own disinhibition coach, we aren't asking you to post a personal sexual trainer at the foot of your bed. Imagine, instead, how some free and encouraging soul that you either know personally or have read about or have seen on the screen, would feel about your inhibitions and what they might say to you to get you to charge through them.

It's fine to have more than one disinhibition coach. You may have one who aids you in expressing yourself in the world or more fully in your relationships, and another who encourages you to try that new position on the bathroom floor, or to tell your partner just what you want them to do with that jar of honey. Who are they? Make a list of some of the things they might say about your sex life right now. Continue to let them have their say mid-coitus, and even allow them to evaluate your sexual performance on an ongoing basis.

Mistaken Ideas

Viv and Mickey are huddled together in a booth at the back of the old time diner on North Street. Viv is sipping on an egg cream soda and Mickey is digging so deeply into his sundae that the fudge and nuts are pooling in a ring around the bottom of the bowl. These two have been coming to the diner together since they were kids. Now that they have kids of their own, it's become a place to get away and hide, just the two of them. Each Wednesday night, they leave their kids with a sitter, while they get their onion rings, ice cream, and the warm delight of a few hours to talk about whatever they want. Tonight the subject is Viv and their daughter Ann's trip to the mall to buy Ann her first bra.

"A much older lady was helping us. She kept looking down her bifocals at Ann's chest and sucking air through her teeth."

"Oh god."

"We finally go away from her and into a changing room. Ann wouldn't let me help her at all, she swore she knew how to put them on."

"Aww."

"When I told her that the cups were too big for her, she told me that her friend Kelly said you needed to buy a bigger bra, or else you'd trap your little breasts and they wouldn't be able to breathe and grow."

"You're kidding me."

"I didn't know whether to laugh or to hug her."

"You know we really have to talk to both of these kids about sex very soon. God knows what their friends are telling them."

"Karen Connelly told me that I could get pregnant from that Navajo blanket in your dad's old truck."

"What?"

"Yep. She said sperm could live for weeks just as long as it was some place warm. And that it was a proven fact that teenage boys were always masturbating into everything: gym socks, towels, and especially sheets and blankets."

"Well she got the masturbating part right."

"Anyway, I don't know if you ever noticed, but I never let us go very far when we were sitting on that blanket. "

"All that time I thought it was because it itched. Okay, I have one. My brother once told me that a vagina has retractable sharp edges, and that if a girl didn't like the way you were doing it, she could just slice your wiener right off."

"Please tell me you didn't believe that."

"I was eight. Of course I did."

"Do you think he was just messing with you?"

"No, he was completely serious. He read all that sci fi as a kid."

"That is so cute that you thought that."

"There are still lots of things I don't understand about sex."

"Oh honey, you know more than enough."

Share the Funny Stuff

The sexual messages that we come across as young people are often as funny as they are rife with shame and prohibition. It can be a liberating experience to share with your partner some of the mistaken ideas you once had about sex. This is something you can do in or outside of the bedroom. It should be good for laughs, some comforting empathy, and it might even infuse your sex with a "look-what-we-can-do-now" boost.

Sit down together with paper and pen and make a list of three funny, scary, or just mistaken things you were taught about sex. Get all the details in. How old were you? What were the circumstances? Did you overhear it or were you talking to someone? How did it affect you and how long did you believe it?

Understanding that you were both curious and foolhardy innocents at one time can help you both connect and feel more open about continuing to unlock the real truths of your sexuality—together.

Forbidden Words

Deidre is wearing her tight new black dress on the dance floor. She has on her best bra and panties, the black lace underwire and matching bikinis. Her hair is down and her sweat adheres wisps of it to her cheeks and neck. Scott is across the floor at the bar. He loves to watch her move like this. He stands and stares, mesmerized like a stranger on his barstool. Finally he puts down his drink and crosses the floor. He needs to touch her. When she sees him coming, Deidre slows to a seductive grind and smiles. Scott slides up to her, grabs her hips, and pulls her to him. The heat is coming off Deidre in waves. She pushes a leg between Scott's and the two of them grind into each other's thighs, unaware of the people around them, consumed with their own chemistry.

"Baby, you look so good," Scott tells her. "You feel *so* good."

Deidre can feel Scott getting hard against her as she presses her chest into his and runs her tongue along the tendons in his neck. Her teeth graze his earlobe and she lets her hot breath tickle his ear. With her eyes closed and the hot rthymn between them as her guide, Deidre licks her lips and whispers, "Take me outside, baby. Fuck me up against the alley wall."

Deidre and Scott have been living together for nine years. They have a child and a history of frustrating sex. Six months ago they decided it was time to start telling each other what they wanted in explicit sexual terms. This meant getting comfortable saying certain words out loud. First, they admitted that there were some words they didn't like. Scott told Deidre he found the word "penis" decidedly un-hot. Deidre said the same was true of "vagina" for her, but "cunt" was a little too scary. They both liked "pussy." Both also liked "breast" and "tits," but "boobs" just made them laugh.

Scary Word Exercise

Part of talking hot is knowing what kind of language works for you and your partner. Sit down together and try the Scary Word exercise. Each of you think about which words you'd like to be able to say and hear from your partner. You can even divide your lists into two columns, one for words you do, and the other for words you don't want used in sex. Trade lists and approve the words you'd both like to try. Now combine the remaining words and say them out loud to each other. Notice how even if you are laughing or getting red-faced, there is a thrill to using those words together. The next time you find yourselves hot and bothered, you'll be better able to start saying so, with just the hot talk that you want.

Freeing Play

When Julie and Sean were first together, their sex was talk-free. They would moan and sigh, but were so intent on pleasing each other and not offending, that a serious tone infused every one of their sexual encounters. Julie thought Sean needed it to be this way. She'd had other male lovers who told her sex was serious. That each time they made love, it was a reflection of their passion for each other. Julie agreed with the passion part, but she also felt that sometimes sex should be light and fun. And she felt that if it could be, she would want to have it even more often. Now that she and Sean had been together for two years, she was confident and comfortable with him, and felt it was high time that they transferred that relaxed attitude to the bedroom.

Sean, for his part, had been afraid that if he did veer away from the heavy connotation they placed on their love-making, Julie would feel less than loved. Sean didn't want Julie to think of him as crass. He didn't want to offend or objectify her. He loved her after all!

One Sunday morning, while Sean was innocently reading, Julie whacked him over the head with her bed pillow. Sean yowled with shock but took the wild grin on Julie's face as an invitation to retaliate, and goosed her ribs until she squirmed away from him and onto the floor. Suddenly, the two of them were wrestling on the remains of their breakfast. Gooey egg yolks and bits of toast and jam were attaching to Julie's butt. She shimmied away from Sean long enough to grab some cold tea and splash it in his face. Sean smushed his palm in the eggs, and smeared the goo in Julie's hair. When they ran out of food, the tickling recommenced until Sean screamed "Uncle!" and they collapsed together in a giggling heap. When they finally raised their drenched and sticky heads, each saw in the other a glow that looked a lot like desire. Julie helped Sean back onto the bed and for the first time, they laughed and chatted their way through some perfectly good, loving, and pretty messy orgasms.

The best sex happens when each of you feels totally accepted as a person. And so to have the ultimate in a good time, you've got to feel free to be playful, silly, and goofy together. Sex almost never goes as perfectly as planned. Many times, the things that go wrong are downright funny. You've got to be used to playing together in other ways before you are sexual, to give yourself a chance at having really great sex. Basically, it's impossible to feel safe being playful while nude when you haven't even gotten good at being playful while clothed! So get ready to get goofy together!

Acting Funny Yourselves

You can start by having some dates where you go to funny movies or plays, or rent a hysterical video. Laughing together at someone else's jokes is a good place to start. And it makes acting like a goof seem okay. Once you have laughed together over someone else's material, it's time to take the big leap into being funny yourselves. If you can't think of ways to be funny and playful together, here are some suggestions:

Take turns contorting your faces like kids trying to gross each other out. Pick someone in your life that drives you both crazy, then take turns doing an out-of-bounds imitation of them. Head to the fridge for a good old-fashioned food fight. Or, if you don't want to stain the room, try decorating each other in absurd food fashions.

Remember, this play does not need to end in sex. It's there to help you realize that it's okay to take each other, yourselves, and your sex less seriously, and be free to be exactly who you are.

Erasing the Guilt

Connor finished taping the fake patch of hair to his bare chest. It was the perfect finishing touch to his seventies high roller costume. His gold chains were nestling nicely against another patch above his belly button, and the pants with the dizzying rows of checks were just tight enough to outline where he placed his package.

When Jennifer came out of the bathroom, she let out a cheer. Connor turned her way and shook his hips and his shoulders.

"That is so great, baby! You look like such a slut."

Jennifer slunk across the room to grab Connor's crotch, but he backed away and froze. The smile faded from his face as he sat down on the edge of the bed.

"What? What did I do?"

Connor looked down and studied the pointy toes of his boots.

"I, uh, haven't been called that in a really long time."

"I didn't mean it. I mean, you look perfect. We're just playing here."

"Yeah, but for some reason it was just strange to hear it out of *your* mouth."

"Why? Who told you you were a slut before?"

"A few people. Remember that girl I told you about—Mandy?"

"The one with the camper van?"

"Yeah. Well, I never actually went out with her, right? I was interested in her friend Delia. Genuinely interested, you know?"

"Uh huh."

"Well, Mandy and Delia and I were with a bunch of other kids at the beach one night and I went off to buy us beer. When I came back, Mandy cornered me by the pier and kissed me."

"Whoa. That's gutsy."

"Yeah, well, then she went back and told the whole crowd. Delia got really hurt and called me a slut and told all of our friends that I was a slut too."

"That's so unfair."

"Right. But that little incident just seemed to follow me everywhere I went. My little sister got wind of it and then she told my mom who actually sat me down and gave me this intense talk. It was all about how I needed to respect girls, and how she was a girl, and if I chose to sleep around with girls that was a reflection of how I felt about her."

"Ooh. Ouch."

"And you know, the thing was, I didn't even want that kiss. I didn't even like it. I stopped it! You know me. I am not a wild man. I'm just a big sap."

"You are honey, it's true. You are the farthest thing from a slut on the planet."

"You think?"

"I know."

Calling Out the Guilt

Imagine taking a journey through your past. Recall all of what you have seen and heard about sex since childhood. Think of your community, conversations with friends, interactions in school, explanations made in Sunday schools or in houses of worship. Think about what you saw on television, in the movies, and on the radio. Think about your own reactions to some of what you heard and saw. What of it made you feel guilty about sex?

Write those guilty messages down and share them with your partner.

Again, take a stroll down your sexual memory lane. This time, think of unspoken messages about sex that came from your family. If your parents did sit you down for a sex talk, remember that. Think of what you heard your parents saying to your siblings about boys, girls, and dating. For most of us, the messages we learned in our families about sex being dirty, shameful, or sinful were probably the most inhibiting. What were your family's major guilty messages about sex?

Write those down and share them with your partner.

Now take some time to explain to each other how you truly feel about all of these messages today. If you can admit that they aren't useful, let each other know why.

You Thought What?

Last week, in the middle of an orgasm, Alex spontaneously slapped Terry's butt. Terry was stunned but not offended. He had had fantasies about being spanked and paddled his entire sexual life. But Alex wouldn't have known this. In fact, Alex didn't mention the slap, just collapsed afterward in a happy thump. When they have talked about their turn-ons, Terry has tried to keep it pretty mainstream. He is afraid of offending Alex, or making him feel like he has to do something that he doesn't want to do. In Terry's mind, they are fine just as they are. They've just celebrated their seven-year anniversary and are finally settling into their first cozy house. Terry knows that eventually they'll talk again about the things that make them hot that they still haven't tried. At that point he'll once more want to bring up the spanking, but he's afraid that he probably won't.

Both Terry and Alex grew up in strict, religious homes. The common sad and funny stories about their Christian and Jewish upbringings are one of the things that helped to bond them together early on. But Terry has never told Alex about the time a nun told him that his dead relatives in heaven were watching him at all times and privy to every private thing he did. This cruel possibility stayed with Terry throughout his childhood and turned early masturbation experiences into guilt-ridden failures. Now, even though he knows better than to give the idea of his grandma peering down at him from a cloud during orgasms much credence, Terry does feel that his sexuality and desires might be offensive to other people—including Alex. Sometimes he thinks he should tell him this story as a way of introducing his fears. It might make telling Alex that he wants more of the light slapping that happened the last time they did it—much more in fact—less of an exercise in fear.

Inhibiting Thought Exercise

Any kind of personal inhibition affects our ability to be comfortable with our own sexuality. The messages that both culture and family can pass on about the inhibition of feelings, of physical expression, even of noisemaking, are important. Sometimes we learn sexual inhibitions in totally non-sexual ways. For example, if Alex has a memory of joyfully dancing to music on the radio, where his mom steps in and tells him to "cut it out," that he is "misbehaving," he may find it very hard to let loose and play later. If you grew up in a family that made you feel you should be "seen and not heard," being fully alive in the sexual experience is more difficult.

On a scale of 1 to 10, with 1 being completely inhibited and 10 utterly uninhibited, how would you rate yourself in your non-sexual relationships? _____ (This measure of inhibition can have a surprising correlation to what happens in the sack.)

Now try to identify the non-sexual messages that you received that told you to be silent.

Cultural messages that told me to be silent were:

Family episodes that taught me to be ashamed of expressing myself were:

Make That Inhibiting Thought Ridiculous

Now that you are more in touch with how inhibited you were taught to be, you can use humor to help break out of it. Create an image of your family or culture's message of repression which is so extreme it makes you laugh. Terry might imagine his grandmother manning a giant telescope from a flying cloud, surrounded by other busybodies who are also too bored in the afterlife to do anything meaningful, and who are in charge of keeping the cloud on a perpetual course over Terry's head.

Share these results with each other and don't be ashamed of having been ashamed! See how you both were at the mercy of early messages? It takes understanding and debunking them to make them fade and to make yourself free.

Naked with the Lights On

"Pair of tens."

"Ah, too bad mister. Four of a kind."

Todd shakes his head, mutters under his breath, and takes off his pants. His plaid boxers feel like nothing on his skin.

"All right, sore sport, you deal."

Todd shuffles the deck and eyes Sally. Her delight is obvious. Her gaze repeats over his bare arms and newly bared feet. He studies that gaze closely, but nothing in her shifts. She obviously likes what she sees.

"Okay," he says, "enough already. Whaddya got?"

Sally leans over like she's sneaking a peak at his hand and kisses Todd full on the lips. Her breasts, which are completely uncovered, scrape across the top of his cards.

"I've got, gee, what do we have here? Looks like it might be, nah, couldn't really be a full house!"

"No way!"

Sally flattens the cards on the sheets before him. Sure enough, she's fanned out a solid full house. Todd swallows hard. Sally begins bouncing on her knees.

"Let's see, buddy. A deal's a deal!"

Todd pulls at the bottom of his T-shirt. They've agreed that whatever happens, he gets to keep it on. Sally is smiling encouragingly at him. He smiles back. What's to fear? He takes a deep breath, gets up on his knees, and pushes the waistband of his boxers down past his penis and balls. He checks Sally. She's looking straight at his dick, same smile on her face. Todd has to lie down to pull the boxers all the way off. Sally helps him with the last pull.

"Beautiful, baby," she says from the edge of the bed. Todd has to fight the impulse to cover himself with his hands. He keeps scrutinizing Sally's face but that joyful look stays in place. It warms his heart when she looks at him like that. He really had no idea that getting naked in front of her would bring out that look.

"Honey," she says gently, "could you roll over?"

Todd closes his eyes and does what she asks. Sally puts a hand on one cheek and kisses the other, then lies with her whole self on top of him.

"I love you, Toddy," she tells him. "You are so beautiful."

Getting Naked Exercise for the Shy

What is happening here is that Todd needs to put his fears of exposing his body to scrutiny behind him, and get some of his feeling of empowerment back. At the same time, Sally needs to feel that he is trying to change, to loosen up. They also need to get some laughter back in their relationship regarding clothing and nakedness. We suggest a game of strip poker (or blackjack, or any other card game), with whoever the shy person is setting the ground rules as to what is the absolute least amount of clothing he/she is willing to wear in the lighted room.

Get out the popcorn and beverages. Get dressed in a special way and agree on the number of articles of clothing each of you will wear. The shy person is then allowed to wear an extra four articles over that number so that they feel more in control. When you get down to your final outfit, if all has gone well, seal the experience with some lovemaking.

The Painful Past

Carl is madly in love with Lucy. His whole life it seems he's been looking for a woman with just her intelligence and grace and warmth. He loves the way she smells, and needs to snuggle into her neck and breathe in her hair before he can fall asleep at night. Making love to her is great, although he doesn't like to focus too much on the sexual side of their relationship. It's the feelings of love and trust that really cement him to her and that are such a relief from the superficial affairs of his past. Currently, talking too much about sex with Lucy seems irrelevant and potentially messy, but he can tell, by the way she has started questioning him about what he wants sexually, that she is sensing his heart isn't completely in it.

When Carl was twelve, he was seduced by a friend of his mother's, a woman in her mid-twenties. Carl hadn't yet learned how to masturbate and was both alarmed and aroused by what was taking place. The sex happened repeatedly during the six months that the woman stayed with his family, always when no one else was home. Carl sensed that he shouldn't tell his parents what was happening, but he did tell his friends, the lot of whom slapped him on the back and congratulated him on his prowess.

One day, Carl's mother came home early and discovered them in his room. She forced her friend to move out and never spoke to her again. She also told Carl he was never to contact her and that they were never to speak of what had happened to anyone else. It took some months before Carl's mother would look him in the eye.

As an adult, Carl knew that sex was important to everyone but felt like it was too often overemphasized and frankly wished that people would just get over what he saw as an obsession with an activity that wasn't always such a great thing. In fact, no matter how much sex Carl had over the years, and he had a lot of it, he never could relax enough to really connect with his lovers. Still, Carl is incredibly attracted to Lucy and there is a part of him that is flattered that Lucy seems to want him and that their sex and his own desires seem to matter to her. If only he could explain how he had learned that a woman wanting him wasn't always a good thing. Maybe then she'd understand his distance.

Sexual Ghosts

Many of us have had sexual experiences in the past that have intensely hurt or frightened us. They follow us around like scary sexual ghosts. Many times we feel that there is something wrong with us because we had these experiences.

It is not really safe to be sexual with someone if you don't feel that you can talk about some of these nasty sexual ghosts. As frightening as it is to open up and risk rejection or not being understood, you need to do it. Your partner needs to be able to be conscious of and responsible with your ghosts. The worst thing in the world is to have painful sexual experiences repeated.

Practice talking about some of your scary sexual ghosts alone. Once you become comfortable with what you want to say, write it down. When a feeling frightens us, even when we've succeeded in putting it into our own words, we can easily forget it later. Write it down. Then, when you feel safe with your partner in the future, you will be able to initiate the conversation about your sexual ghosts and fears.

How to Make Some Noise

Jack is the silent type. He'll talk when he has to, but always with his words chosen carefully and his demeanor distanced and respectful. This part of his personality affords him a certain freedom; his friends and coworkers consider him beyond reproach. At home with Laurie is the one place that Jack does express his opinions. "Laurie's great," he'll say. "Lets me get things off my chest, shares a lot of my interests. A very comfortable and understanding woman."

By all accounts Laurie and Jack really do get along very well, which is part of the reason Laurie is averse to telling Jack one very sensitive thing—that she is ready, after many years of his silence in the sack, for him to make some noise. Their sex is warm and regular. Laurie loves how desired Jack makes her feel, the way he heats up in her hands, and the way he always asks her, after he's come, if she'd like anything more. The one thing that Laurie would truly like is to hear what Jack is feeling *during* sex. She doesn't need a play-by-play, or even for him to come straight out and verbalize it, she'd just like to hear him moan a bit, mutter a curse word or two, maybe let her name slip from his lips. She knows that part of the problem is Jack's punitive upbringing, where emotional expression of any kind was discouraged. So she sits him down gently after a day spent gardening to try a freeing little exercise. She offers to give him a full-body massage.

Jack is pleased and lays bareback on the bed under Laurie. As she presses into his shoulders, then runs her hands along his lats, his breathing gets labored.

"Is that okay?" she asks him.

"Yes, good," he tells her, barely able to get the words out before she pushes the heels of her hands into his lower back. As she works, Laurie continues to ask him how he's feeling, until Jack is finally so far under the spell of her touch that he can only moan his responses.

"You know what?" she says. "You just keep letting me know it's working with those moans, and I'll stop pestering you."

That is how, forty-five minutes later, Jack, for the first time in all of his forty-five years, moans his way through an erection, a blow job, and the most relaxed ejaculation of his life.

Sexual Voice Exercise

Whether one of you is as quiet as Jack, or you just want to be able to sound off louder and more often when things are feeling good, the point of this simple exercise is to find your voice when you are receiving pleasure. Set aside some time to be alone and relaxed. Have your partner give you a long, slow foot rub. As you are feeling the pleasure of the foot rub, work at saying the ooohs and ahhhs that you usually don't voice.

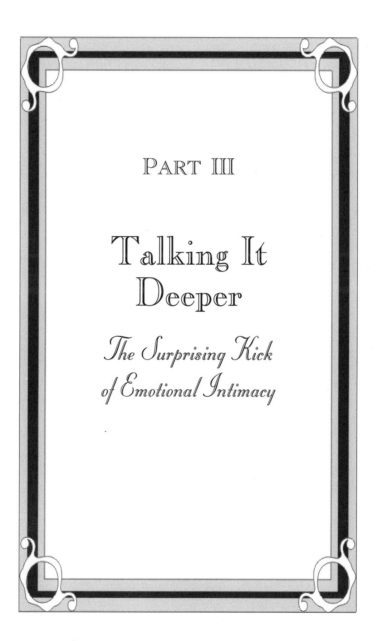

PART III

Talking It Deeper

The Surprising Kick of Emotional Intimacy

Hot Harmonies

Monica left work early. She was bristling again at her boss's insulting behavior, and by two in the afternoon she just had to get out of there. She sat on her bed at home swearing under her breath. She was a grown woman for god's sake, and a consummate professional. Not to mention the mother of three, whose first son was years older than this blowhard she had to answer to on the job. When Jess got home, she was still steaming.

"Hello, hello!"

"Hi, Dad," the girls answered from the front room.

"Come back here," she thought, "and put your arms around me."

"Where's your mom?"

"We dunno."

Monica drew a breath and listened closely, willing Jess's footsteps down the hall. When he opened the bedroom door, she was sitting on the edge of the mattress, smiling thinly up at him.

"Hello, gorgeous," he said as she rose to hug him. "How's my favorite creature?"

Monica rested her cheek against his chest and sighed. "I've been better."

"Ahh. Well, whatever happened, it left you looking good."

"Thanks."

"Mmm. And smelling good. And feeling awfully good. What's going on?"

"It's work again."

"Aha, Heir Junior."

"Yessss."

"I'm telling you, you really need to reconsider my sugar in the SUV tank idea."

"Maybe I need to reconsider the whole job."

"You're great at that job. Really, Monica, you shouldn't let that guy take that away from you. He may be a crappy manager, but that shouldn't mean the end of you getting what you want."

Monica sat back on the bed and let Jess's words wash over her. He was right, she knew. If she could remove her despicable boss from her job, she would be pretty content. Maybe she just needed to get better at ignoring him and concentrating on herself. Monica felt a surge of relief. Leave it to Jess to help her out. He was such a blessing. She ran a hand along his back and hugged him tighter.

"Which is you."

"What?"

"I want you."

"Oh sweetie, you have me. Come here." Monica kicked off her shoes and she and Jess stretched out on the bed. "You are good at so many things. That guy just can't handle having such a competent and undeniably hot employee."

"Oh right."

"You think I'm kidding? You gotta feel sorry for him really. I'd go crazy if you worked for me."

"Rest assured, Jess, that'd never happen. You would be working for me." Monica snuggled closer and ran her hand up Jess's thigh.

"Anything you say, boss woman."

Harmonic Convergence

Sex and intimacy are related, but they are not the same thing. You can have fun sex without emotional intimacy and you can have emotional intimacy with someone you love, and avoid being sexual with them. We want you to experience the pleasure of having both with the same person. Sex and intimacy are both very powerful on their own but put them together and hold on to your hat! In a good relationship, sex is like very powerful cement, gluing you to each other even tighter.

The best sex you can ever have happens when your relationship is harmonious. The trick is to get close to each other emotionally, and then stay close. Falling in love is magical, but that's just the beginning of a relationship. We know a lot more now about what it takes for couples to make it in the world together than we did a few decades ago. For more information about this, check our Resources section for the books of Gottman, Notarious, and Markman, which contain in-depth analyses of successful long-term couples.

One of the most important things researchers have realized about successful couples is that they have a very high ratio of positive to negative interactions. A five-to-one ratio to be exact. When you say or do many, many more positive than negative things to your partner, that partner feels close to you, like you are squarely on their side, or as if you are their best friend. Maintaining this goal of emotional closeness is an important ingredient in your motivation to be physically close.

Notice how Jess was able to diffuse Monica's stress and anger with his love, compliments, and reassurance. And how they were both going to come together sexually to finally get through and past Monica's upset.

The goal of the following exercise is to come up with a list of kind and positive things you can do for or say to your partner. Your goal here is not necessarily to end in sex, but to create and/or reinforce a loving atmosphere that will help emotional and physical closeness thrive.

Write these positive things down and then follow through by saying or doing some of what you've proposed. And remember, even when this exercise is finished, to always keep that five-to-one ratio in mind.

Positive things I can say to my partner about him/her in general are:

Positive things I can say to my partner about him/her sexually are:

Positive things I can do for my partner today are:

Now take some time to think about when you will make these positive gestures toward your partner. What's your deadline date?

What You Still Love About Your Sex

Nate has spent the last month fuming that Mel has not wanted to have sex. "I'm sorry," she's said to him. "I just don't have the energy right now." Sometimes she substitutes "these days" for "right now." The last time she said it, he told her she should just come right out and say "ever again." Immediately after that though, he felt bad.

Part of him did understand. She was back in school. The kids were being difficult. And ever since the merger, her job seemed to keep changing. But he missed her. And he missed sex!

Nate knew that she felt he was being cruel. She had that distant, self-protecting look on her face whenever she talked to him now. That just made him feel worse. Maybe, if he could explain to her that he just wanted to be close to her and have sex once in a while—not all the time like she probably thought—that look on her face would go away.

He found her reading in bed. It was a Friday night and she was reading a novel, not one of her business school books. He sat down on his side of the bed and touched her hair.

"Can I talk to you for a minute?"

Mel rolled over and put her book down. "Okay," she said.

"Look, I realize I've been kind of a jerk about sex. I know you have tons of stuff to do right now and it probably seems like one more demand on your time, my asking for sex."

"It's that I wouldn't be any good. I'm so distracted with all this stuff. I'd be tired and cranky and wouldn't be able to focus. Do you understand?"

"Yes, yes, I do. But you've always said that sex helps you relax. Don't you think you could look at it that way?"

"I don't know."

"Look, I can be better at it."

"Better at what?"

"Better at sex. I can make it better for you. More relaxing."

"Okay, wait a minute. This really is not about you being a bad lover. I want you to understand. Are you listening? This is about my doing a million things at once. You think that I don't miss the sex?"

"Yes."

"Well, you're wrong. I do."

"What do you miss?"

"God, you are such a goof. Come here."

Nate slides over, lays his head on Mel's pillow, and blinks up at her. He's starting to feel better. Mel grabs a handful of his collar and pretends to strangle him.

"I miss the way you feel, numskull. Your touch. The way you talk to me when you're working your way down my body. I miss the look on your face when you come. And, you're right, I miss how relaxed I feel afterward."

"Mmmm."

"What do you miss?"

"What do *I* miss? How much time do you have?"

Reconnecting Exercise

When relations get tense and disconnected as a result of the stress and strain in your day-to-day lives, resentments can build and eventually wreak havoc with your sex life. When either of you is feeling sexually disconnected, find a quiet space and time and sit down together. Each of you take three to five minutes to silently think about the way your sexual relationship has been going recently. Even if you are angry or upset or feel rejected by your partner in some way, there are parts of the sexual encounter that you must still have good feelings about. Focus on the things that you know will be relatively easy for your partner to give you. In your mind, make a list of three things you still like in your sexual relationship. When you are done with your lists, take turns sharing aloud and do your best to make real eye contact. Once one of you shares, the other should repeat back what he/she heard, then receive the positive information. Do not take this time to add on negative information or in any way take the positive charge away from this shared experience. Simply say "thank you" each time you are told that your partner likes something you have done in the past.

Secret Passageways

"Uhh."

"It's okay sweetie, go ahead."

"It's just that . . ."

"I know. But I wanna know, really."

"You go first."

"Okay."

"No, no, I'm sorry. I'll go."

"All right."

"So, are you sure you want to hear this? Well, if it doesn't make sense to you or anything, just let me know."

"Okay, I promise."

"Blah. Okay. I want to learn how to last longer, you know, not come so quickly. And I want to be able to get hard again real soon after coming and be able to do more stuff and then feel what it would be like to come twice. You know, at least twice."

"Maybe even more than twice?"

"Maybe, you know, but I'm not asking to be Superman."

"Right."

"Okay, now you go."

"Um. I want to be able to give direction. In the middle of sex, I mean. I want to be able to know what I want to happen next and then tell you or even somehow just shove us into place and make it happen, instead of you having to decide all the time."

"Really?"

"Yes. Is that all right?"

"Well, yeah, I'd love that."

"You would?"

"Well, sure. It would feel more like, I don't know, you really wanted it. I'd like that."

"I was afraid it might offend you somehow."

"No. It doesn't."

"So, that's my goal then. But I don't know that I'll be able to do it right away. So, don't look for it to happen the next time we have sex or you might be disappointed."

"Yeah, me neither actually. Don't expect me to instantly become porn star man."

"Don't worry, I won't."

"I'm kind of embarrassed, you know. That I've been having sex all these years and I have so little control over my dick."

"I know what you mean. How can I be this old and still not be able to ask for what I want? It feels pathetic."

"Well, honey, your secret is safe with me."

"Yours too."

"Should we start trying to do these right away?"

"Like I said, I'm not sure. Maybe just when we feel ready."

"Okay, right. No pressure."

"Yes."

"This could be good though, you know."

"Yep, I think so too."

Secret Goal Exercises

Each of us has something, or several things, that we would like to change about the way we relate sexually. It might be liking a part of our body more than we do, or being able to function differently, like lasting longer or becoming easily orgasmic. Often, we feel shy, or upset, or ashamed about our own goals. Maybe we're worried that we might never be able to meet them. Maybe we're worried that if we tell our partner, they will want those things for us too, and hound us about them. So often we don't even share these secrets about how we, ourselves, want to change. This is a chance to do that.

Each of you write one or more secret goals you have had about ways you want to change sexually.

Person A wants to change in these ways:

Person B wants to change in these ways:

Share what you have written and talk about the reasons it is frightening to share the goal(s) with your partner. Tell your partner the truth about being "afraid you'll hound me, or afraid I won't be able to do it, or afraid I'll feel terrible because I can't function the way I want to." Then each of you promise the other that you will not use this information in any way that is hurtful.

What Not to Say

Jarred was gaining his strength back after coming. He was still turned on from Sherry's blow job and ready to be inside her.

"Are ya ready?"

"Not quite. I think I need you to go down on me again."

"What do you think I was doing for that whole twenty minutes?"

"Excuse me?"

"Nothing, forget it."

"Listen buddy, choking on you for half an hour is no picnic either."

"Well, at least it ends with a prize."

"You call swallowing that swill a prize?"

"Hey, at least you don't have to put your tongue in traction for nothing."

Zero Zingers Exercise

Lots of times, what you want in your sexual relationship involves treading on some pretty sensitive territory. Because of culturally enforced myths and anti-sexual socialization, most of us are pretty defensive when it comes to our own sexuality, especially when we are asking for things in the heat of the sexual moment. Emotions can run high, and hackles can rise. So what do you do when you or your partner wants to change or add or ask for something sexual in midstream? Well, to begin with, if intimate sex is your goal, then your immediate strategy in talking is not to be brutally honest. To have any sexual communication be effective, your partner must be able to hear what you are saying. You can see, in the example above, that starting out with reactionary criticism about the sex just doesn't get this guy where he wants to go.

The goal of this exercise is for you to become consciously aware of the things you might say to your partner which will cause them immediate pain or distress, *and to avoid saying them.*

> In private, on a separate sheet of paper, make the following lists for yourself:
>
> Things that I could criticize about my partner's sexual skills or tastes which would really hurt him or her:
>
> Things I could tell my partner about my other partners which would really threaten him or her:
>
> Things I could criticize about my partner's body which would wound him or her:
>
> Things I could remind my partner about his or her past sexual behavior which would really shame him/her:

Okay, now that you have this very important list, your goal is *not* to bring up these topics casually, on the spur of the moment, during a sexual interlude, or when you are angry. Some of them would be best never said. Others, which are relevant to your pleasure and connection together, need to be said carefully, during times of closeness.

When You Make Me Feel Bad

Jay lays the last pancake on Tricia's plate and reaches back to turn off the burner.

"Thanks, these are good."

"No problem."

"First I get great morning sex. Then I get fed. I love Sundays."

"You thought the sex was great?"

"Well yeah, you didn't?"

"Um, no, it was good, you know, really good. Only . . ."

"Did I make too much noise again?"

"No. Huh? No. I wasn't even thinking about that. I think I'm over that, really."

"Then what?"

"You laughed."

"I laughed."

"Yeah. You laughed when I first pushed inside of you. You said, 'Are you in yet?' and then you laughed."

"Well, I wasn't sure and it seemed kind of funny that I wouldn't know."

"Yeah, I get it. But I felt pretty embarrassed. Like I was so small and my being small was a joke of some kind. I feel pretty sensitive about that kind of thing, really."

"Oh, Jay, I'm sorry. You are not small in my book. I mean, I guess I thought you already knew that. It was just that you weren't hard yet, remember? It would make sense that I couldn't feel you."

"That's true."

"But look, I'm sorry anyway. I can see how that would have stung. You're plenty big, mister. You don't hear me complaining when I'm making all that racket do you?"

"No, you don't sound too unhappy."

"I'm sorry, hon. I feel bad about laughing. I didn't mean it in that way at all."

"Yeah, okay."

"Here, sit. Wanna help me eat the last one?"

How I Feel Exercise

Over time, it is inevitable that you and your partner will hurt each other's sexual feelings. One of the important things that marital researchers Gottman, Notarious, and Markman (see Resources) have found is that positive couples' communication is made up of a lot of "I" statements. Now, you may have heard about the importance of making "I" statements before. But they become especially important when discussing sex: an arena where you would really have to be a mind reader to get through all the layers of inhibition and expectation to arrive at what your partner means before they have a chance to tell you. We cannot emphasize enough how important it is not to do "mind reading," and start out attributing bad motives to your partner for something they are doing that you don't like.

Think of a time that your partner either did something sexually that you didn't like and that hurt your feelings, or didn't do something that you wanted and hurt your feelings in that way. Write down an "I feel" statement that states your feelings of hurt, but does not criticize or zing the other person, or assume that he or she meant to hurt you. The purpose of this exercise is not to place blame but to foster positive communication about sensitive sexual feelings of uneasiness. The next time you find yourself in such a situation, talk from that "I feel" place, and see if you don't feel better about how you express your discomfort.

Captivating Closeness

Roger and Jose were still buzzing from their night out. They'd discovered that a fabulous chocolate souffle had been added to the permanent menu of Jose's favorite French restaurant—a place they hadn't set foot in together for close to a year. Both of them tossed their jackets on the hall table and jokingly waddled up the stairs to lay their full bellies down in bed. Before the threshold to the bedroom, Jose stopped them, took Robert's hand, and smiled shyly into his happy eyes.

"Thanks for tonight. I've missed you, you know?"

"I know, honey, me too. Come on."

Roger led them to the bed, sat Jose down, and kneeled behind him.

"What say we trade some massage until there's room enough in our stomachs for something more?"

Jose laughed and leaned back into Roger's kneading hands. "Tonight is only the beginning," he thought to himself. "We keep this up and we'll be fine."

Roger's hands worked down from Jose's shoulders. When they reached his lower back Jose moaned and rolled himself flat out before Roger. Thoughts of Tony and Billy's breakup flared then faded under the hypnotizing strokes of Roger's fingers. They both had been so frightened when Tony had sat them down and explained how a five-year commitment can dissolve just like that. When they left Tony's house that night, Roger cried all the way home.

"We are just like them, you know," he had said, as they pulled into the drive.

"No we're not."

"We are. So busy with work and our individual friends. We're never together anymore. Aside from the house stuff and the random dinner at your mother's, we barely talk."

"I know, but the love is there. It is."

"When was the last time we had sex?"

"Oh, I don't know."

"You see? We have grown apart. I don't want that, do you?"

"No, of course not. But sometimes life gets in the way."

"So? We don't have to let it always be in the way. That's what happened to them. They forgot what was important."

"Come on. Do you really think that was it?"

"Partly. Let's promise each other, right now, that we will spend more time together."

"Okay you, I promise."

"Me too."

"Me too ..." Jose mumbled as Roger's fingers dug into his hamstrings.

"What, honey?"

"Mm. Nothing. I was just thinking about us."

"Yeah?"

Jose rose up, pushed Roger down, and straddled his hips for a little reciprocal rubbing.

"Yeah."

"God that feels great." Roger sighed as Jose pressed his hands into his shoulder muscles.

"You feel great," said Jose, leaning down and kissing Roger's ear. Roger wiggled his hips underneath Jose.

"And you, my dear, feel ready for something more." Jose rolled off Roger and laughed.

"Bring it on, mister. Bring it on."

Closeness Check-in

Good sex thrives in an atmosphere of consistent closeness. If you spend a good part of your time avoiding your partner, connecting sexually will not be as fulfilling as it could. This is an exercise in making sure that you and your partner are both on the same page when it comes to feeling emotionally connected to each other. On a scale of 1 to 10, with 10 being very connected, and 1 being very disconnected, write down how you feel toward your partner this week.

Person A Score: _____

Person B Score: _____

On a scale of 1 to 10, how connected have you felt toward your partner this month?

Person A Score: _____

Person B Score: _____

If your scores are consistently 8 and above, give each other a hug and yourselves a pat on the back. You have done an enviable job of staying close lately. If any of your scores are below an 8, complete the following exercise:

Write down something small your partner could do to help you feel closer to him or her.

Person A: ____

Person B: ____

Jointly agree on a time to talk about these ways to feel more connected. Discuss the issue until you each have agreed on something sweet and meaningful for your partner which you are willing to do. Put this plan into action during the next three days.

Reconnecting by Noticing

Angie rolled the cart past the mint cookies a second time. No. No. Definitely no. We do not need these in our house. She flashed on Randy gobbling them down. He liked to eat them one right after another. He would stuff the small disks into his mouth whole and moan ecstatically with each chocolate-coated bite.

"Oh, what the hell," she muttered, and laid the box atop a bag of artichokes.

As she drove the sedan along the last few curves before the house, she marveled that there were no drained juice bottles rolling beneath the seat. There were also no crumb-filled paper towels or browning apple cores skittering across the dash. Randy never nagged her to clean this car. He just opened all the doors on the weekend, plugged in the wet-dry vac, and did it himself.

"My man," she said aloud. He could be a dolt, for sure. What, for instance, does any person over forty need with a knee-deep collection of domestic beer bottle caps? But these things he did for her. Without being asked. And without, in most cases, even being thanked. These were what he was really about.

She would thank him when she saw him later. Or maybe she'd just hold the cookies under his nose and back the both of them into the bedroom.

Conscious Noticing Exercise

Sometimes couples lose sight of what each of them does (or doesn't do) to maintain the emotional connection. This is an opportunity to tell your partner what he or she is doing right. Make a pact for the next week that you will each pay attention to what your partner is doing that is right. Now, this may actually make each of you act nicer toward each other, and that's all right. Set a time for a week down the road to exchange information. At that point, give each other a list of three things the other person did that made you feel most loved. During this exercise, simply receive the information, say thank you, and write it down. You will probably be surprised by some of what you hear. The things you did purposely to please your partner may not have been noticed, while things you didn't know you were doing may have been treasured! Simply write down the positive information you receive and thank your partner.

Advanced Exercise: Missed Gifts

This is an addition to the above exercise that, although ultimately helpful, does have the potential to expose feelings of resentment and disappointment. Please only venture ahead with it when the two of you are feeling safe and connected. And remember that in simply taking the time and making the commitment to do these exercises together, your partner is proving that he or she has the strength and the willpower to make things right between you.

The goal of this exercise is to share the information about the things each of you tried to do to be loving during the week which were not received or treasured by your partner. Remember that you also have information about what you did that did make your partner feel loved. In other words, this is an exercise in empathy—in learning how your partner really reacts to what you say or do, not how you imagine they would or should react to you.

When you are in a safe and quiet place together, take turns in sharing what you intentionally did to be nice to your partner that she or he did not even notice. It is all right to say that you were disappointed that your gift wasn't appreciated, but it isn't all right to be angry or accusing.

Use this exercise to reframe things for each other. Put the emphasis on the fact that these are merely miscommunications between you, and that there are things in your partner's behavior which each of you really do value.

The Den of Romance

Last week, on a train ride home, Charles was deeply moved by a few lines of poetry that the city's art council had postered in the train. It was a part of a love sonnet written by Rainer Maria Rilke. Charles took out his pen, scribbled the words into his day planner, and read them to Cleo after dinner that night. They were both so inspired by the poetry that they went down to the den, where their own tiny collection of poetry was housed, and leafed through for more romantic stuff.

While Charles poured them a drink, Cleo pulled out their copy of Pablo Neruda's *Twenty Love Songs: And a Song of Despair*. They settled into the couch, pulled an afghan over their knees and began to read aloud to each other. As they kept reading, the words seemed to fill the air around them with the ache and possibility of true love. When they finally closed the book, their drinks were drained and they were each close to tears. They peeled off their clothes right there on the old cracked sofa. It was a heady and passionate session of lovemaking.

Tonight they are going to revisit the den. This time with a romantic, erotic film, and food and drinks that could as easily be drunk and eaten off each other as from the coffee table. Love is now alive in their basement!

Tuning into Romance

It is one thing to take each other out for a romantic night, but how do you distract yourselves from the routine distances of a life in your cluttered home and create your own den of romance? Take some time to discover what each of you feels you could do (or have done) at home that feels romantic, and that sets the stage for lovemaking. For example, talking about scenes in movies and books can be a good way to communicate what you like in sex and relationships. When you take that a step further and actually watch the films together or read to one another from those books, the night's romantic fate can be sealed.

Set the stage for your romantic night in. Pare down the clothing, warm up your room, dim your lights, and make sensual food and drinks (exotic mixed drinks or erotic-looking non-alcoholic drinks with fizzy mineral water and a slice of fruit cut just so). Have your books chosen and before you, or your movies rented. Some viewing suggestions include:

Last Tango in Paris

An Affair to Remember

American Gigolo

The Way We Were

The Lover

Henry and June

Frankie and Johnny

Mississippi Masala

Kama Sutra

The Good Kiss

Michelle and Darrell each love kissing. There was a time, however, when they were not very fond of kissing each other. Michelle suspected that part of the reason for this was that they had such different kissing styles. Her kiss was light and affectionate, which Darrell interpreted as chaste and boring. Darrell, on the other hand, liked to pry Michelle's mouth open with his tongue every time he got near her. This made Michelle feel like she was back in junior high, and had an over-eager sex fiend for a grown-up boyfriend.

One day, when Darrell leaned across the kitchen table to give Michelle half a piece of the gum resting between his teeth, she bit it off, kissed him, and licked the sugar off his lips. His groin stirred. Darrell looked at her for a second, startled.

"That was really nice," he said, and leaned in to gently kiss her back, first on her bottom and then her top lip.

"Mmmm," she said, cocking her head to the side and closing her eyes. "Very nice."

They leaned in together again and Michelle pushed both their lips open with her tongue and stole the gum from Darrell's mouth. Darrell laughed, took her face in his hands, and stole it back.

These days, Darrell and Michelle like to improvise their kisses. Sometimes blending a series of kisses from their expanded repertoire. Their kissing seals them to each other as they start their days. It keeps them sensually connected even when they are not being sexual. And it makes their foreplay more fun.

Recipe for Good Kissers

There are lots of couples who aren't on the same page when it comes to ideas about the perfect kiss, but we think many of them are much too scared to discuss and process the differences. People tend to kiss in a very automatic way. Over time, couples tend to stop experimenting. There are zillions of ways to kiss. This exercise is fun, and if you process it as you go along, just focusing on expressing what you like, you will wind up with more ingredients in your sexy kiss recipe.

1. Give each other a soft kiss. How do you each like it?

2. Give each other a hard kiss. How do you each like it?

3. Give each other a kiss with lips closed. How do you each like it?

4. Give each other a kiss with lips parted. How do you each like it?

5. Give each other a kiss with your mouth open. How do you each like it?

6. Give each other an opening and closing kiss with no tongue touching. How do you each like it?

7. Do a kiss with medium tongue action. How do you each like it?

8. Take a delicious candy and pass it back and forth as you kiss. How do you each like it?

9. Do a kiss with little nibbles. How do you each like it?

10. Do a kiss where you suck on one another's lips. How do you each like it?

PART IV

Obstacle
Course for
Lovers

Getting Over and Under
What's Holding You Back

The Great Dane

Emma is close to coming. She can feel herself going slippery as Adam's tongue works her clit. Her fist closes around a tuft of his hair and her butt muscles tighten. "That's it," she thinks, as the orgasm begins to wind its slow way up through her body. She opens her eyes to look down at Adam and catches a glimpse of her mother's birthday gift, wrapped, and still on her desk. "Oh, damn, I never mailed that thing." Adam keeps working deftly away and even moaning a bit in anticipation of Emma's coming. But she's lost it. She tries to cover by tightening her butt muscles again and sighing deeply. "Feels good," she tells herself. "Almost there." Why that's the same thing she said to herself when she was working out on Monday. Today's what, Saturday? Adam shifts his approach and adds two fingers to the mix. "Come on, girl," she tells herself. "Concentrate."

Taking the Great Dane for a Walk

Men and women are different sexually in some very important ways. One of them is that once aroused, men have what is called "the point of ejaculatory inevitability." That means that at a certain point in a man's arousal, he will be able to orgasm, pretty much no matter what else comes into his head. He could have a fleeting thought about his taxes being due, what a pain his boss is, his son needing lessons on how to drive a car, or his need for a fresh haircut, but these thoughts would not be enough to prevent him from ejaculating. This accounts for why more men than women consider sex to be "relaxing." No matter how stressed men are, once the point of ejaculatory inevitability is reached, their physical release is assured.

Women, on the other hand, are much more distractible. It can sometimes be more work for women than men to become aroused in the first place, and it is certainly more difficult for women to stay aroused. There is no point of inevitable orgasm for women. Instead, women can get distracted and lose their arousal at any point in the sexual encounter. Once arousal is lost, women need to start to build their arousal all over again from the beginning. This is why coauthor Aline always encourages women to think of pursuing their own arousal and orgasm as if they were "Taking a Great Dane for a Walk." If orgasm is a woman's goal, she has to take control of her sexuality and her thoughts and not let her unconscious wander. Just imagine that you are becoming very aroused, and then visualize stopping yourself from getting caught up in a thought about the details for a presentation you will be making the next day. You need to be talking sex to yourself and nothing else. You need to grab that Great Dane and yank it back on the path to sexual pleasure.

The Great Dane exercise is an exercise in self-awareness, communication, and self-control. First, write down all of the things that you believe are bothering you enough to distract you during your sexual time together.

Secondly, before you get into the sexual situation, briefly describe all your potential concerns and distractions to your partner. (Partners should listen sympathetically, but problems need not be solved at this point.) Thirdly, promise yourself that when distracting thoughts come up, you'll yank on your own chain and get that Great Dane right on track.

Sex Night

Corrinne and Daniel look like they've finally managed it. They are in bed, undressing each other under the covers, getting lost in their happy and familiar chemistry. There are those smells of their skin and hair, and here's the neck biting they've always loved. Here comes the hard, needy grind of their thighs and groins. The possessive squeeze of hands gripping each other's asses.

Corrinne stops David for a second and grins at him.

"What bliss is this?"

It's not even ten o'clock The kids are asleep. Their own bellies are quiet but not too full. And when they close their eyes, the sexy softcore images of the cable show they just watched are still flashing.

Just a week ago a dalliance like this would have seemed like a pipe dream to these two. It's not that they had zero "adult" time. In fact, since their two-year-old Melinda was born, they'd learned the lesson of creating the time and space to be alone. That space became a Friday night, twice a month, where they'd meet friends for food and drinks, and stay out late enough to feel like something more than young parents. But when they'd finally collapse into bed, sex would inevitably be a quick event. Both of them might be assured of a fast, little orgasm, but rarely anything more.

When their friends called to suggest a new watering hole a few days back, it dawned on Daniel that what he and Corrinne really needed was a night devoted to seduction. They'd still see their friends, but how about marking a separate night on their calendar just for some slow sex? Eat with the kids. Put them to bed at a decent hour. Turn on some Al Green or a film with some risque scenes to put them in the mood. When Daniel first suggested it to Corrinne, she wasn't so sure.

"Do you really think that'll work? I don't know. Seems nice, don't get me wrong. But it also seems kind of artificial. Who knows if we'll be in the mood?"

"You just get some good sleep these next few days," he told her. "And we'll see how it goes."

Now, as they wriggle out of the last of their clothes and Corrinne rises up to throw a mounting leg over Daniel, he reaches for her breasts and stares up at her.

"How do you think it's going so far?"

"So far? Hmmm . . ." Corrinne winks at Daniel as she lowers herself down. "So far, I'd say, sooo good."

Sex Night for Parents: An Exercise for People with Small Kids

Couples with small children who don't have really close relatives nearby have difficulty finding time for great sex. Women have a more difficult time than men, because of their arousal patterns and because they frequently have primary responsibility for childcare. It takes a good night of sleep to be able to be a good parent in the morning. And it takes a long time of lovemaking for many women to click off from the mommy role and remember that they are sexual beings.

Even if you are a very social couple, make a joint decision that sometimes you two will have to forego "social night" with other people for "really steamy sex night" with yourselves. Most couples really cannot have both of these fun activities in the same night. Ahead of time, take out your calendars and mark off one or two (or more) weekend nights a month where you will not make plans with other people. No family obligations, no anniversary dinners, no movies and dinners with friends. Make a plan for the day of the date night that includes:

No cooking or cleaning up of the evening meal. Get takeout or heat something up.

Feed the children and get them to bed early.

Eat dinner early yourselves. Again, do not fuss with cooking or cleanup.

Do not answer the phone after six o'clock.

Have a home movie or something fun to watch at home while you wait for the kids to settle down and go to sleep. Whatever this is, make sure you are doing it together.

You will have digested food and gotten your children to sleep by nine o'clock.

You will now have at least two hours to have prolonged sex, to do one of our exercises, or to just lay down and enjoy each other's bodies. All this, and you will still be able to get to sleep early enough to enjoy being a parent the next day.

Body Image Banter

Stacy and John were making love with their pocket Kama Sutra lying open next to them on the dresser. They had talked the previous night about growing tired of their limited repertoire of positions, and this morning took their first, trembling trip to the sex toy store. As soon as they got back, they climbed into bed with the book and selected the afternoon's new position together. They were ready to improve on their standard missionary, which they'd come to vary over the years only by the different bend or lift of Stacy's legs. And they'd decided that their occasional doggie-style move, which only seemed to happen if they had extra time, or, come to think of it, when all the lights were off, was just not variation enough. This time, Stacy was straddling John, her hands on his collarbone, his on her breasts. The depth of penetration had them proceeding gently at first, but soon it was feeling just right and Stacy smiled hugely down on John, anxious to lock eyes when she came.

John, for his part, was busy looking at Stacy's body, taking in the newness of this position. He loved the way he could see her rising and falling on him. He wanted to burn the image on his brain. To his surprise, Stacy suddenly lost the rhythm and stopped. She slid off him and onto on her side.

"Baby, what happened?"

"I don't think I can do that, John."

"Why, did it hurt?"

"No . . . No. It's just, I can't. Okay?"

John wasn't going to force Stacy either to try it again or to talk, and when she slid under him and pulled him back inside her, he went along and kissed her full on the lips. He moved slowly between her legs and managed to keep the questions out of his voice. "I love you, baby," he said, from his familiar place on top.

Can you guess what happened here? Stacy did feel like she couldn't keep going on top of John, but not because it felt uncomfortable or was tiring her out. Stacy stopped because she realized her body was being exposed. Her belly was rising and falling with her breasts, her thighs squishing thicker with their contact with John's chest. When they did it the old way with her flat on her back, Stacy felt like her bad parts were minimized. This new way made her feel fat and, as John looked over her body like that, repulsive.

John, on the other hand, thought Stacy looked pretty damn good. He's always loved the curve of her belly, and the drape of her thighs doesn't really bother him. Truth be told, thinking about any part of her looking bad was the last thing on his mind. He was distressed that just when he thought they were finally making progress, finally going to incorporate a new, promising position into their sex life, she wanted to stop. And he didn't know how to get her to tell him why. John felt a little frustrated and very lost.

Like many people, Stacy has body image issues that play a significant part in her willingness to try new things. Studies show that women who view their bodies negatively are "less interested in making love . . . more restricted in their range of sexual activities, and [have] more difficulty becoming aroused and reaching orgasm" (Love 1999). And such a large majority of women view their bodies negatively! The numbers of men who are beginning to feel the same way about their own bodies is on the rise. It is very important for both partners to be sensitive to each other's body image fears. The more you can engage in loving body image banter with a cringing lover, the closer you'll come to freeing both of you up.

The Body Comfort Trinity

First, denounce the big body image myth:

Lots of people, women especially, are operating under the misconception that their lover is turned on or off based on how she looks. The truth of the matter is, studies find it is how a lover "responds" sexually, not how he or she looks, that makes them sexually attractive and memorable to their lover.

Second, talk about that response:

Talk out, or, if you need to get clear first, write out, all the ways in which you value your partner sexually. What does he or she do that feels especially good? How does he or she react to what you do that feels especially good?

And third, talk about what *is* attractive to you about your partner's body:

What are those aspects you enjoy? The way he moves his hips? The heat that comes off her skin? The way he smells when he starts to sweat? That curve right there? The slide of that bone over here?

The more you are able to understand that your sexuality goes far beyond your looks, and the more comfortable your partner feels about your appreciation of him or her as a responsive lover, the more you can both understand and get comfortable with the whole of sexual attraction and motivation. And once you've mastered the elusive state of body comfort, think of how many new, comfortable contortions lay ahead of you!

You Sexy Naked Thing

"I get hard just looking at you," Philip said. And it was true. Sharon was innocently changing out of her work clothes and into her nightgown, when she looked in the mirrored closet doors and saw Philip's bulge through his pants. She slipped slowly out of her underwear and stood there, one hand on her hip, the other bunching the nightgown into a ball. Philip touched himself through his pants, while taking all of her in. The cushiony curves of her large, heavy breasts and wide, sensuous hips; the short, soft brown hair that accentuated the graceful connect of her neck and shoulders; the slide of her solid back into her sweet plump ass; and the way her thighs, with their softest skins, touched there at the top, as if just waiting to be parted by his face and hands.

Sharon smiled teasingly at Philip, put her hands through the armholes of the nightgown and raised it overhead. "Nooooo!" he moaned. She laughed, finally throwing it on the floor and climbing on top of him.

Philip had been telling Sharon how beautiful she was since they'd first met. Back then Sharon begged to differ. She thought she was fat. She wore a size fourteen, and explained to Philip that all her life she'd been tortured by images of conventionally "sexy" women. The billboards and magazines were in agreement—beauty was thin waisted and skinny legged, with firm, high breasts and flat stomachs. Even the skin mags and porn films Sharon had seen confirmed it—albeit with somewhat bigger breasts and hair.

Philip tried to explain to Sharon that those folks had it all wrong. One day he even stood her in front of the mirrored doors and showed her. He thoroughly traced her body with his fingers and gave a running commentary of what he touched. "I feel like I could suck on those breasts forever. They are so soft and warm and full. See? They make me crazy . . . Notice the way your ass rises right there? And that part of your lower back makes that shape? Like an arrow pointing down? That is so hot!"

Sharon had felt a little shaky when Philip first stood her up, but soon she was laughing and blushing and covering his hands with hers to join him on the journey. When they reached her thighs, her warmly complemented knees went weak, and she had to sit down. Philip was right, she knew. Her ampleness could be very sexy. She vowed then never to forget the way the tour of her own body made her feel.

Take a Body Tour

Over 90 percent of women report feeling worse about themselves after paging through women's magazines. And men these days are growing more critical about their bodies in large numbers. As always, the size of their penises continues to be anxiety producing for many men, but now, chest size, amounts of body hair, height and weight are becoming problem areas too. By helping yourself and your lover forget about irrelevant cultural messages about beauty and discovering your unique brands of sexiness, your reward will be freer, hotter sex. Start now by taking a talking tour of each other's bodies.

Stand up, lie down, kneel. Feel free to move around as the tour demands. You might want to have a hand-held mirror ready for those hard to reach places. As your partner tells you about your body, don't contradict or thank. Just absorb what they're saying and let them do their thing. When they're finished, return the favor.

If this exercise sounds overwhelming or you have reasonable concerns that your lover may use the opportunity to be critical, you can also take the talking tour yourself. Stand in front of a mirror and proceed slowly, using your own hands and eyes. Feel the warmth of your neck, the tickle of your arm hairs, the thankful curve of your belly. Your entire self is capable of great sensual feeling and expression. Celebrate the gorgeous body that takes you there!

Picky Eater

Ronnie was a little embarrassed standing there in the tub with Peter peeking up between her legs. Luckily, he was being gentle and good humored about this whole washing thing. He ran the washcloth softly back and forth over her labia, then paused, put his nose to her, and sniffed.

"Well?"

"Yum," he said. "Like roses."

Last week Ronnie and Peter had an enormous fight about how little oral sex Ronnie gets. While Ronnie has been giving Peter blow jobs six ways till Sunday, every single time they have sex, Peter just rubs and rubs and rubs on her with his fingers before they fuck. This is something that never makes Ronnie come, and sometimes barely makes her wet enough to take him inside her. "If you would only use your friggin' tongue," she screamed at him, "it would make all the difference in the world!"

Luckily, this fight happened the night before an appointment with their therapist. The therapy sessions had been scheduled to help them resolve some tensions that had resulted from Peter's elderly mother's recent move into their house. Ronnie was still so steamed about the fight when they got to the office that she didn't even let the therapist proceed with their weekly check-in.

"Why should I be the primary caretaker for a woman who can't stand me when her selfish son won't even condescend to give me a little head?!"

Peter glared at Ronnie for a few seconds and then turned to the therapist.

"I don't give my wife oral sex because she smells."

Before Ronnie could finish hatching a plan to kill him, the therapist asked them if they'd thought of ways to address the smell. If they had ever tried, for instance, bathing together before sex. They both just blinked at her. She smiled.

"Give it a try," she said. "It worked wonders for another couple I know."

Picky Eater Exercise

Consider the difference between a picky eater and a good eater. For every food you now enjoy, there was a first time you tried it, not knowing whether you would like it or not. But you took the leap. Maybe your mom or dad coached you to try it as a kid. Maybe you decided to try it again as an adult when your tastes matured.

Lots of us now like some pretty weird foods, and come up with even weirder food combinations. You were brave to try the hairy kiwi fruit and the raw fish startle of sushi. If none of us had taken risks with food, our only culinary experiences would be breast milk, formula, and pureed foods. So hooray for taking risks! Of course, the difference between becoming a "good eater" and developing an appetite for all kinds of delicious sexual tidbits is that sex is still thought of as dirty in our society. It's a lot harder to experiment with sex than it is with food. There is certainly no one standing at the end of your grocer's aisle offering you mint condoms on a toothpick.

Both of you make a list here of your old sexual stand-bys, the sexual equivalents of spaghetti and sauce, chocolate milk, and applesauce. Now make a list of the sexual foods you have seen or heard about that you haven't had the nerve to try, yet they intrigue you. Make a few visits to the sexual supermarket (see the chapter on Shopping for Sex) to get help with even more ideas, then re-make your foods-to-try list. When you're finished, give yourselves a "try it" date. Be adventurous. Cherry-flavored lube can turn anything into dessert.

The Panda Syndrome

Cedric has found the bootleg tape he made back in '64 of Ella Fitzgerald at Radio City. It was the very same night that he and Cherise met. The tape is a bit crackly and it fades in spots, but Ella's velvet voice still manages to fill the room and embrace them both. Cherise is massaging Cedric and her touch sweeps and dances with the swell of the music. In addition to their soundtrack, they've bought some warming erotic oils with an intoxicatingly light, musky smell. As Cherise rubs it into Cedric's chest and belly, it heats both their skins. "Honey, that is lovely stuff," he says.

Cherise pours more oil in her hand, rubs her palms together and suspends them over his stomach once more.

"What do you think?" she asks.

"I think that's about enough," Cedric says. "Though that sure felt good. I will definitely sleep tonight!"

Cherise gets up and rinses off her hands, turns off Ella, and returns to lay down beside Cedric. She kisses him lightly on the shoulder and pulls the covers up around them. Cedric is already drifting off to sleep.

"Good night, my dear," he murmurs.

"Good night."

Overcoming the Panda Syndrome

This is an exercise for the literally millions of couples out there who are very loving with each other but just keep avoiding sex. Picture a male and female panda. They are cuddly, adorable, and peaceful. You can picture them cavorting happily about and eating bamboo. But it is almost impossible to get them to mate!

It is not uncommon to find some very wonderful but sexless couples these days who secretly have the "Panda Syndrome." Their friends have no idea that they are not sexual partners. They seem so perfect together. They are friendly, loving, respectful, and affectionate, and they work and play with enthusiasm and cooperation. But they have no sexual relationship. It's not always clear how the pattern of avoiding genital contact started, but once the pattern of being loving and affectionate but nonsexual starts, it is difficult to stop. We can help you break the Panda Syndrome.

1. First, agree that you want to begin to become sexual partners again. It must be a joint decision.

2. Each of you, if you haven't already, have a medical evaluation to make sure that the pattern is not a result of a medical issue you are avoiding which can be treated, like a pain disorder or erectile problems. Also, consider the idea of whether or not you might want to see a sex therapist for an evaluation.

3. The next step is to look at your behavior together and talk about the kinds of touching you have been doing that you each now evaluate as "normal" and "non-sexual." For some couples with the Pandra Syndrome, kissing, and even genital touching, has become "non-sexual," because you have evolved into a pattern where it is understood by each of you that these touches will not progress to sexual excitement. At this point, it is almost impossible for either

of you to signal to the other that you want to resume being fully sexual.

4. Talk about each of your thoughts about how and why you each drifted into the Panda Syndrome. Share your thoughts and ideas about your sexual history together, and discuss the ways in which not being sexual has become normalized.

5. Next, begin to incorporate some new behaviors and signals into your behavior together—signs to both of you that you want to create sexual excitement. One place that you may want to begin is with some special eye-gazing exercises. Try the book, *The Art of Sexual Ecstasy* (Anand and Hussey 1991); it has some excellent practices. You can also try the complementary sexual reawakening exercises in *Acupressure for Lovers* (Gach 1995) (see Resources).

6. Set up a defined time twice a week when you will be trying out new behavior. Begin building up feelings which you both define as erotic, electric, and arousing. Agree that any touch you undertake after these new activities is going to lead to sexual pleasure and sexual activity. Have fun!

In Your Own Hands

Maggie laid the vibrator down on the bed and pulled at her underwear. She held her breath and listened for sounds from the rest of the house. Nothing. Her kids wouldn't be home for at least another hour. She really was alone. She kicked free of her panties, pulled the comforter back up to her chin, and smiled. She couldn't help herself. The "shoulder massager" was the best gift her sister had ever given her. Maggie reached for it again, closed her eyes, and pressed the vibrating head lightly to her clit. When the vibrations got too intense, she lifted it away. Maggie had some time. She would take this one slowly.

With the vibrator buzzing in her right hand, Maggie ran her left hand over her stomach and traced her nails under her breast. Yep, this felt great. She sighed and relaxed her whole body. Her fantasies were starting. Maggie could start to see another couple. They were doing it doggie style as she looked on through their bedroom window. Maggie kneaded her breast then ground her nipple between her fingers. She moved the vibrator to the tops of her thighs.

The woman in Maggie's fantasy was dirty blond, her breasts large and swinging as her lover pounded her from behind. Maggie concentrated on those breasts as she reached for the vibrator's g-spot attachment. She ran the curved top up and down her labia, then eased it through her vulvar opening and against the front of her pelvic wall. The man in her fantasy was starting to moan. He was unsteady on his feet, gripping the blonde's ass as she bucked him back.

Maggie began tensing her own ass and rising to meet the vibrator head. With her left hand she started working the attachment, shoving it against her front wall until she could feel her g-spot start to engorge. She was so close now, and her fantasy couple were already coming simultaneously. Maggie saw past them to the neighbors where a man had knelt in front of his lover and taken his hard penis into his mouth. She saw the kneeling man jerk at his own penis as his lover's shaft slid in and out of his wet lips. There was a look of ecstasy on the standing man's face. As she pounded herself and rose hard against the vibrator, Maggie saw the couples discover each other, locking their eyes as their orgasms began to break. She came with them, one muffled cry for their four fantasy howls.

Masturbation as Inspiration

There is an old school of thought that masturbation within a relationship takes away from a couple's sex life. Some people still believe that masturbation is like stealing from the sexual energy that exists between two people. They think that if a partner is able to satisfy her/himself alone, that partner depletes the sexual energy necessary for couples' sex, or is in fact indicating a disinterest in her/his partner by choosing to masturbate at all. However, today's view is much changed from this idea. Unless a partner is masturbating excessively, to the point where there is no sexual interaction with a present partner, masturbation in fact most often helps a relationship. Masturbation can help us to relax about sex, it can keep us focused on what it is that we really want (or want to try), by reminding us what our fantasies are and what kind of touch we like. And it can keep us more in touch with our own sexuality, with the idea that we like to feel good, which in turn keeps us interested in a sexual life with our partner.

When we masturbate, we teach ourselves valuable sexual lessons. Some women like Maggie learn that they need steady clitoral stimulation to come. They might also discover that they do indeed have a working g-spot or that they like their nipples squeezed nice and hard. A man might learn what kind of touch, pressure, and speed work best for him, and he might discover that instead of being done after one orgasm, he loves the feeling of going for two. When he can take his time, the almost ticklish sensation of being spent after coming will give way to a new level of intensity that is out of this world. Both genders may learn which images make them hot, even which positions or scenarios they might want to try.

Some of us may have been masturbating for as long as we can remember but no longer do it regularly or even see it as necessary in the context of a relationship. Masturbation, however, is a great way to get reacquainted with what you really want, at any time in your life.

If you have never masturbated, now is the time. Try to do it privately at first. Mutual masturbation is great, but you need to be alone to really get acquainted with your own pleasure. A pair of hands, of course, is all that's needed for either gender to begin. Some women who have trouble achieving orgasm through manual stimulation are able to do so by using vibrators, dildos, and other sex toys. Other women say that certain shower settings aimed straight at their clitoris also work like magic. Men report that certain fabrics sometimes feel better against their penis than their own hand. Experiment! Lubrication and music without commercial interruptions can enhance the experience for anyone.

To find vibrators and sex toys that are right for both men and women, we recommend the helpful and discreet retailers listed in our Resources section in the back of the book.

Strictly Stereotypes

Urban dwellers Sarah and Michelle are young and in love. They are also each so sensitive about not asking for sex unless they are sure that the other one is horny, that they now get down to it about once a month—a lot less often than they would like.

Sarah and Michelle's neighbors, Steve and Rachel, are still bristling from the fight they had after counting up their previous sex partners for each other. It turns out Rachel has Steve beat, by nearly two to one. Now he's silently steaming and seriously reconsidering those fantasies he'd been having about marriage and kids.

Steve's friend Joe is trying to come up with a good excuse to leave his colleague's dinner party early. Janet rejected his advances this afternoon and he can't bear being at a table with her surrounded by happy couples. He's certain none of these men have his sexual problems. He feels like a hideous failure.

True or False?

____ If a woman wants sex a lot, there is a good chance that she'll cheat, not be capable of true love, and be a distracted and unequal partner, a bad friend, and a negligent parent.

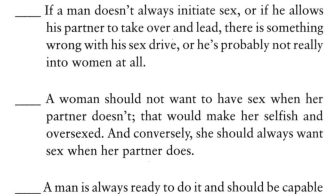

_____ If a man doesn't always initiate sex, or if he allows his partner to take over and lead, there is something wrong with his sex drive, or he's probably not really into women at all.

_____ A woman should not want to have sex when her partner doesn't; that would make her selfish and oversexed. And conversely, she should always want sex when her partner does.

_____ A man is always ready to do it and should be capable of turning his partner on at any time.

Obviously, each of the above statements is outrageously untrue and deserving of a great big "F." But can you see how they are related to the three very real situations described at the beginning of this chapter? Gender-based sex myths do a great deal of damage, often on a subconscious level. They reinforce unnecessary and rudimentary stereotypes and can be hugely influential, even among people who pride themselves on knowing better.

Sex myths related to gender often do have very real consequences, and can be especially dangerous if they are not debunked. If Steve, for instance, is not able to tell Rachel, "I'm afraid if you have had this much sex, you will never be satisfied with just me," and instead lets his fear and embarrassment simmer, he may just choose to walk away from a perfectly good opportunity at lasting love. If Steve could understand that he is at the mercy of a myth, and discuss this with Rachel, he could hear that in fact she has only ever been truly satisfied with him. Rachel has been looking for a man like Steve all of her adult life. Her past was about experimentation, not true love. Furthermore, she never cheated on any of those lovers, so that will not have to be a legitimate concern for Steve either.

Think about whether you are affected by any of the myths listed above. Do you feel this way deep down? Do you suspect that your partner might?

Myths into Mincemeat

1. Sit together and write down the sex and gender myths that affect you. Be honest. Try to go beyond the short list we've created, and come up with some of your own. Leave some space on the page after each myth.

2. Now, under the myth, write the practical effect it has on your sex life, your feelings of love, and your feelings of self-worth and confidence.

3. Take a break now and discuss what you've written with each other. Are you both affected by the same myths? Can you agree that they have no practical purpose in your relationship?

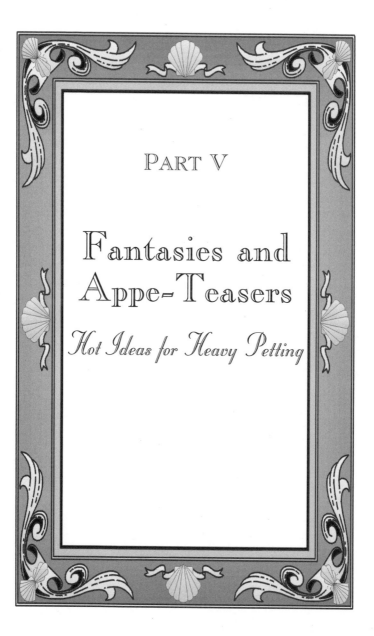

PART V

Fantasies and
Appe-Teasers

Hot Ideas for Heavy Petting

Rebel Yell

Every time Gordon's little brother takes a vacation, Gordon nabs the guy's cop uniform, billy club, and cuffs. He is too tall for the getup, but it fits Lucia beautifully. Lucia has even bought a pair of black workman's boots especially to match.

Once she's donned the uniform, she is no longer Lucia, but "Officer." Gordon has learned the hard way that "yes, Officer," are the only two words he need utter in response to her commands. Usually if he does everything she says, his "arrest" (for any sort of bad behavior that the Officer deems punishable) ends with him cuffed to the bed post, the mean Officer's uniform's coat tails rubbing his belly and thighs as she rides him. Once, when he didn't obey, he was cuffed to the closet door handle across the room and forced to watch Lucia pleasure herself with the billy club, far out of touching or tasting range.

Flaunting Authority Exercise

Is there anyone out there who doesn't like to rebel against authority? This is an exercise for you rebels out there. Rebellion, authority, and sex make a wonderful trinity, given sex's place in the forbidden zone.

Take some time to think about the "forbidders" in your life. Some of them will be very personal, like your cruel gym teacher or your mean Aunt Ellie. Find out from each other all of the things you each felt forbidden to do at various times in your life—both sexual and nonsexual. Make a list, if you like.

Once you've gotten in touch with what's forbidden to you, this exercise has many variations. Playing like one of you is a figure of authority (a police officer, FBI agent, sexy dominatrix, nun, or priest), and the other one a naughty miscreant, can be great fun. Many of these fantasies are universal and don't need much explaining—what would an authority figure say and do to a miscreant and how could that miscreant appeal to the figure to dole out the punishment? Is there a way you can get yourselves a uniform? Anything in your own closets that would suffice?

If you choose to make it a more personal fantasy by rebelling against a particular relative, neighbor, or teacher, the exercise is more idiosyncratic. You have to explain your past for your partner. You have to share with your partner the kinds of things the "forbidder" said to you, the tone they used, and any other essential aspects of their personality and appearance, so that your partner can successfully mimic them. Are they angry because you were eating with your fingers today? Wearing too much makeup? Swearing? Get as serious or as silly as you want to be.

The Good Teacher

Sondra leans back against the pillows and pulls at Thomas until he's sitting astride her.

"Here," she says, pressing a finger to her lower lip. "Start here."

Thomas kisses her bottom lip, gently runs his tongue along the length of it, then catches it softly between his teeth. Sondra then pulls back from him and runs a hand roughly through his hair.

"Now both lips, and use your tongue again."

Thomas does what he's told, licking Sondra's top and bottom lips in a slow circle. He then presses his own lips into hers. Sondra sighs and kisses him back, allowing his eager tongue to dart into her mouth.

Thomas wants very much to lay Sondra down and climb on top of her for some deep kissing, but he knows better. He kisses her hard and awaits further instruction. The heat of her and his own helpless anticipation is giving him quite a rise.

Sondra pulls her hair off her neck and piles it on the pillows behind her. She unbuttons her shirt and opens it just the slightest bit.

"Now work your way down to my breasts from my neck."

Thomas can see Sondra's cleavage and the hook of her bra as he goes for her neck. Instinctively, he reaches a hand inside her shirt. She jerks back and surveys him harshly.

"Uh, no," she says. "I never said anything about hands."

"Sorry, miss."

Thomas feels slightly humiliated as his hard-on rages. Sondra senses his dilemma and decides to give a little. She runs her hands down the front of his shirt before yanking it free of his pants. She then runs her nails back and forth over the top of his belt and raises her right thigh, pressing firmly against his groin.

"Jesus, Sondra."

Next Sondra pulls a single breast free of her bra, and Thomas smothers it in kisses.

"Now suck on my nipple, gently at first, then whip your tongue back and forth a bit . . . that's it, now bite, softly . . . oh yeah, you got it."

Classroom Exercise

Good teachers, apart from being tantalizing authority figures, are also able to impart critical knowledge to their students. In this exercise, the partner who is assuming the role of the teacher is not only playing with power and anticipation, she is also teaching her partner what she likes. Whether you want to offer some very detailed sexual instruction to your partner, or you both like the dynamic of playing with control, the classroom exercise will serve you well.

Remember as you progress in your roles (one as teacher, the other student) that the student knows very little about the subject and needs to be given constant and clear instruction throughout the exercise. Also, remember that teachers are ultimately gentle and well-meaning and want their students to perform well, and that students are often hesitant, insecure, and eager to please. Good luck, students and teachers. May you both make the grade!

The Bookstore Blowout

Jill and Eddie's "free ideas nights" all started by accident. They arrived at their favorite restaurant on a Wednesday night, only to find that there was a convention in town and they couldn't be seated for an hour. They decided to kill some of that time at the bookstore across the street. This store was known for its comfortable sofas and hands-off sales staff. It was the perfect place to wait. Once inside, Jill made a bee line for a big, velvety love seat and plopped the picture book on the table beside her into her lap. When Eddie joined her, he took one look at the cover and laughed.

"Nice choice, honey."

Jill had chosen a giant, illustrated sex manual. She hurriedly cracked it open, so passersby couldn't read the huge S-E-X screaming from the cover, only to find that each page featured a blown-up photo of naked couples in unimaginable contortions.

Soon Jill and Eddie's fascination got the better of them and they leafed through the pages slowly, studying the bend and balance of the poses, and smiling at each other like conspirators. They skipped dinner that night and were so light-headed after their raucous bout of post-bookstore sex that they learned to eat first and browse the shelves of their favorite bookstore section second.

Going Out for a Hot Read

Want a cheap date that can spice up your sex life? You'll need about six hours for this plan. Think of a location that has an interesting and appealing restaurant near a large bookstore. You'll want a store with lots of plush seating, or maybe a coffee bar. Check ahead to find the hours of the store; it is important to be able to spend several hours there if you want. Plan a night to go to the area, have an early dinner, and have plenty of time to spare.

You are on a "shopping trip" together, one that doesn't need to but could result in purchases. Head to the self-help/sexuality section of the bookstore. There are books on fantasy, books with great pictures, and books with new ideas about things you might want to try together. Load up on what looks interesting and find your seats together. Each of you should bring to your seats whichever books contained the pictures or ideas that stimulate you. Read or show each other what you have found that appeals. Make a mental note of any ideas you like. Purchase any books that are just too good to pass up. Go home and put your new ideas into practice.

Talking About Them

"He's bi. On Fridays he goes out with his girlfriend, Susie, who's a coed at State. She likes him because he's sensitive and has a beautiful dick. He likes her because she screams when she comes and isn't afraid to use a strap-on."

"Okay, all right. And on Saturdays he has dinner with his boyfriend, Michael. Michael makes him sumptuous feasts then ties him up with velvet ropes and eats dessert off his naked stomach."

"What do you think he's reading?"

"*How to Land a Cheerleader: A Guide for the Unathletic Male.*"

"No, no. Something by Anne Rice."

"Yeah. *Interview with a Really Hot Vampire and His Sister.*"

"Good one."

"Okay, there he goes."

"He's moving kind of slowly."

"Yep, he's sore."

"All righty then. How about her?"

"Who?"

"The waitress with the braids."

"Can you see her name tag from here?"

"Cherry."

"No way!"

"That's what it says."

"Wow. Okay. She's really a madam and dominatrix who works a few shifts here to keep the cops off her tail."

"She has memorized the entire Kama Sutra and can perform fellatio underwater for a full four minutes. She likes to cuddle but despairs of ever finding a partner who could love her despite what she does."

"When she gets off work, she'll go to the apartment of a steady client whom she calls 'Mouse.' She'll grab her whip, chains, nipple clamps, and gags, which are in a bulging briefcase she keeps in the trunk of her sensible sedan."

"She'll have changed in the car. Latex cat suit. Stiletto heels. Her hair in a tight ponytail. When Mouse opens the door, she'll kick him to his knees and force him to lick the heel of her shoe."

"See, now you're turning me on again."

"Check please!"

What They Do

You probably know this already. Because sex is so private, you can't judge very much about the bedroom habits of another from their outward appearance. That staid professor you see walking around the library with a stack of books in her hands might be an uninhibited vixen in bed. The traffic cop you see during rush hour might actually like to be manacled to his bed by his wife. By keeping this in mind and engaging your sexual imaginations, taking a simple walk down the street together can be an exercise in mutual sexual titillation.

Caution: Don't do this exercise if either one of you is insecure enough to feel threatened by your partner singling out a cute man or woman. Or modify it by agreeing to choose only those people you assume your partner will not find threatening.

Plan to take a walk together someplace where the people watching is good. Pick a place that appeals to both of you. It could be a crowded beach, a mall, a museum, a café, a park, a ball game, whatever you like. On the chosen day, go to your venue dressed in a way that makes you feel attractive and sexy yourself. Walk around or sit together holding hands. Scan the crowd for someone who piques your imagination. Squeeze your partner's hand, whisper who it is, and start to share your story of their steamy sex life.

Dressing for Undressing

Shelly's mother had given her a loose V-neck angora sweater for her fiftieth birthday. It was a little big and bright red, the kind of color Shelly would only wear to a holiday party or an especially conventional business meeting. But she found herself drawn to it because it really was the softest material, and it kept her surprisingly warm. Tonight was the second night in a row that she'd worn it to the dinner table. Every time she reached for a dish to pass, the sweater's loose neck bared one of her shoulders. By the time she'd finished her salad, she'd given up on straightening it altogether and ate the rest of her meal with her bra strap showing. Their home-from-college daughter could care less about the state of her mother's sweater, but each time Shelly looked over at her husband he raised an eyebrow.

Later, when the daughter had run out to another of her many social engagements and Shelly and her husband had finished clearing all the dishes to the kitchen, Shelly put her feet up on her daughter's abandoned chair, closed her eyes, and began to lift her arms overhead for a stretch. Out of nowhere she felt her husband's hands on her. He reached inside the sweater to cup a breast and spoke hotly into her ear. "God, Shel, you are driving me crazy in that sweater."

Shelly was so surprised that she laughed out loud.

"This baggy thing is turning you on?"

"Oh yes. Come on, come with me to bed. But leave it on, okay?"

Clothing Cues Exercise

When identifying to your partner what you find attractive or sensual or sexual about them, you also want to look for clues in their dress and comportment. Try thinking outside of the box here. In Japan, the bare neck is considered an object of desire, very much like cleavage is in the West. Clothes that accentuate or display a certain body part can become your tools of attraction and seduction, and it's important that each of you lets your partner know how you feel. What are your own special likes and dislikes in this arena? Try to pay attention to what your partner is wearing or how they're wearing it and give them specifics. "I love it when you wear that low-cut shirt that bares your neck and lets me see your collarbone," for example.

Some of our associations with clothing and comportment are based on good (and bad) experiences we have had earlier in our lives. One woman may love the sight of her partner in a cardigan sweater, while for another it makes her feel that he has become a little old man. Now, that partner is under no obligation to stop wearing his sweater. But, if he's in the mood to spark something, he'll know the cardigan is an obstacle.

You can send more signals to each other with your clothed bodies, both in public and in private, then you realize. It may be that your shiny hair is a terrific turn-on, particularly when it is newly shampooed. Is it a short skirt and painted nails, or flowing cotton pants and a face free of makeup, that draws your partner in? Maybe you love it when he wears the pajamas that drop below the crack in his ass. Or perhaps there's something about the sight of him dressed up in a suit that makes you weak. There is important information here, and once you get it and give it, you both can use it to flirt shamelessly at home and in public. All you have to do is approach your partner, lower your voice, and ask how they like what you're wearing, or if they're interested in smelling you. Give one another the information needed to stir each of your desires, and watch the clothes you love to see each other in come on . . . and off.

Fantasy Us

"You had just come back from running. I remember because I was only starting to wake up and the first thing I saw when I opened my eyes was you through the bathroom door, stripping in front of the shower. You were flushed from head to toe and your hair and skin were shining with sweat and your breathing hadn't quieted yet, so your chest was rising and falling fast and your breasts sort of quivering. You looked so strong and sleek and capable of doing all kinds of things to me with that athletic energy of yours. I could feel my morning hard-on start to ache, and really, I wasn't going to say anything, just grab ahold of it and take care of myself while watching you soap up behind the shower glass. But then you turned to step into the tub and your back and your ass were so beautiful and I didn't mean to but I moaned."

"It was almost a cry. I thought you might still be dreaming."

"It was like a dream. The way you looked back at me and saw what I was doing and started to smile. Then you turned off the water and strode toward me like that."

"You looked nice and desperate."

"I was desperate! And when you climbed on top of me and grabbed my hand off my dick and tied my wrists to the post like that and your wet skin started sliding against mine and your breast was dangling above my mouth—Jesus, it was turning into a very good dream."

"You are making me wet, honey. Remind me, what happened next?"

What happened next was Yvonne and Rod began to kiss and move against each other while Rod continued telling their story. When he got to the part where Yvonne was bucking on top of him, they found themselves in a heated recreation of that part of the scene.

Talking the Fantasy

Talking about fantasies can be a wonderful part of a couple's sex life. But many couples keep their fantasies from each other out of fear. They assume that their partner will be offended, or are afraid that the partner will feel that they want to actually realize the fantasy, when they really just want to keep it in their head. The vast majority of us do have fantasies, and we use them! It is believed that many women have a deliberate fantasy playing out in their mind during lovemaking. And that this fantasy is the one way they are able to become aroused enough to achieve orgasm.

You may not want to plunge right in and confess a particularly hot fantasy that excludes your partner if you are concerned about how she/he will react. However, there is a nice, safe way to introduce shared fantasies into your relationship. Make a point to do what Yvonne and Rod happened upon naturally here: talk through a yummy sexual memory of your very own.

You needn't agree on the chosen memory beforehand. Just get comfortable and let one person start talking. Hearing a lover recount his/her turn-on with you creates an amazing sexual charge, and remembering yourselves having good sex is great for mutual sexual inspiration. One person can tell the whole story or you can take turns. Just remember to keep it hot and to stay close when you're talking. This is one exercise that may inspire you to play along.

The Ban

Ali and Joan make the most of sexual anticipation. They love to give one another massages, and they'll kiss and scrape their nails over every inch of each other's beautiful skin for hours before attending to their genitals. Ali has even studied tantric sex to try and prolong his orgasm. He's found that it has also helped him shift his attention away from his penis and onto how good the rest of his body feels when Joan is touching him, and what magic it is to touch all of Joan. These two have come to value the electricity that runs between them just as highly, if not more highly, than their orgasms. Lately, they have taken their love of anticipation even further and instituted a full-on intercourse ban. On a "ban" evening, their mutual seduction can go on for hours, involving anything they please, but intercourse itself is not allowed before eleven o'clock.

Their last "ban" night started with a shower before dinner. They let the water run enough to steam and warm up the bathroom, then each took turns soaping the other up by hand. No washcloths or scrubs, just the firm and loving touch of fingers over every inch of each other's skin. Ali got hard while he was soaping Joan from behind, and she teasingly backed up into him. But they quickly separated, rinsed, and with sensual and tickling strokes, dried each other off. Joan put on a garter and thigh-high stockings and Ali donned the tight V-neck sweater and subtle scented oil that Joan loves so much. They went to their favorite Caribbean restaurant, squeezed together into one side of a darkened booth, and fed each other their salads and entrees. By the time dessert arrived, Joan's left leg was wrapped around Ali's right, and he was running his fingers under the garter's straps, and his roughened knuckles along the bare flesh of her upper thighs.

When they finally paid the bill, Joan was more than ready to head home and resurrect Ali's hard-on, but it was still only 9:30. After a make-out session on the curb that nearly broke both of their resolves, they opted for taking their energy to a neighboring dance club. The club was fairly empty and the DJ was appealing to the few couples there by shamelessly playing Marvin Gaye and Barry White. Joan and Ali found themselves in a heated, slow-moving embrace that was too much. They retired to the bar and teased each other with kisses and ear nibbles until it was time to go.

Their electricity carried over into the car ride home, with free hands slipping under shirts and into pants. A flustered Joan honked the horn when Ali sucked too hard on her neck. When they finally crossed the threshold, the wall clock read 10:45. Down on the floor across from the clock they went, licking and sucking and fingering and teasing until, yes, finally, the little hand snapped solidly on the eleven, and the sound of a single condom packet tearing open resounded through the room.

Enacting the Ban

The ban is a fun and effective way to use anticipation and build up heat in a relationship. Again, you want to make sure that you are emotionally close to and trust your partner, so that the ban is a mutually agreed upon activity and not a tease. The ban is an exercise that has to be agreed upon by both of you, and it needs to be a ban on an activity you both desire. Talk clearly about what that activity would be.

You can decide to ban certain kinds of touching, certain kinds of activities, or certain body parts. The goal is to create as much sexual excitement as you can without breaking the ban. This can mean keeping the ban going for a few hours, a whole weekend, or a week. The ban works to heighten sexual pleasure for several reasons. It provides a change of pace; it builds up the excitement derived from ultimately doing something forbidden; it encourages a couple to be creative in their giving and receiving of sexual pleasure; and it increases your ability to avoid linear, goal directed sex, i.e., kissing ➤ touching ➤ genital touching ➤ oral sex ➤ intercourse.

All You Can Eat Special

Denise piled the sex toys at the far end of the table. Abe, who was standing in front of the chocolate and whipped cream centerpiece, lit the lavender candles. "What a feast," Denise said as she stepped back and surveyed the spread. "Wherever do we start?"

Abe laughed and strode to the head of the table. He closed his eyes and reached a hand into the first of three waiting salad bowls. Denise came over to him and they both bent down to read the slip of paper in the candlelight. "One full minute of kissing with tongue," it read.

Abe let the paper waft down to the floor and took Denise's face in his hands. "You time us," he said.

When they were both weak-kneed from the kissing, Denise selected another slip from the same bowl. She smiled and backed away from Abe, sat on the edge of the table, and began to slowly unbutton her shirt. "Yes!" Abe shouted. "My slow striptease with shirt and bra!"

Sex as Salad Bar Exercise

One of coauthor Aline's patients, who was distressed that his wife didn't want to have as much sex as he did, expressed his frustration by saying, "I thought that sex in marriage would be like an all-you-can-eat salad bar!"

Many men and some women fantasize about sexual banquets of unending variety, which fit into their lives seamlessly, despite other relationship and scheduling difficulties, family obligations, or a partner's exhaustion or illness. As unrealistic as this is, the idea of an all-you-can-eat sexual salad bar is nevertheless a good one. It just needs to be tempered with the reality that most of us aren't able to stomach one every day. Instead, we need to create a spread for ourselves when we both have the inclination and the time.

The goal of this activity is to create a freewheeling sexual experience with guaranteed pleasure and some extra special surprises. And to eat as much as you can!

First, clear some time in your schedules. Second, clear a table of all clutter. Now, arrange three bowls on the table. Label them "Appe-teasers," "Main Courses," and "Desserts."

For the ingredients, each of you write down your favorite sexual and sensual activities on separate sheets of paper. Focus on things you really like being done to you, or those you like doing to your partner. If there are activities that are a source of conflict, don't include them in this exercise. Try to think of those things that turn you on, and extend your pleasure, as well as whatever really works as a "main course." Be as specific as you possibly can. For example, "two minutes of gentle kissing on my neck" might be one entry, and "one minute of kissing on my thigh" another. After you've written your entries, fold them in half and place them in their appropriate bowls. Also add to the table any appropriate props: sex toys, whipped cream, oils or perfumes, candles, or foods for mutual feedings.

Prepare yourselves a comfortable place to lie down together, or one that accommodates your favorite or even a new position. Let it be fairly close to your salad bar. Now, go to the table, and taking turns, start eating your way through all three courses. Bon appetit!

The Guided Striptease

Will takes another sip of water and turns around to face Donnelle. She flips on the soul station and sits back in the chair. Her eyes stay on him as she crosses one ankle over the other on top of the ottoman and smiles.

"Your hat please."

Will grabs the ski cap off his head in a quick jerk, flings it across the room, and gives Donnelle a smoldering look. She laughs as she catches the hat and spins it on her finger.

"Okay now, that big silly coat."

Will rolls his right shoulder seductively free of the jacket's sleeve, does a little spin, and shakes his hips as he peels the other arm out. Donnelle is laughing hard now as he strolls over, lays the coat on her lap, and kisses her full on the lips.

"Off with your shirt," she growls at him and pushes him away.

Will straddles the ottoman and grinds into her shins as he slowly frees his shirt buttons, one after another, until all are undone and he can run a hand along bare skin from his neck to his belt.

"Mmm, very nice," Donnelle tells him as he spreads the shirt open wide.

Will yanks the shirt all the way off, stripper-spins it overhead, then shimmies farther up Donelle's body and lassoes her head between the long white sleeves.

"You are not done, mister. Get back there and lose those pants."

Will is having a hard time controlling his laughter, but he backs off and faces her from behind the ottoman. The belt comes off with a zing and Will whips the air with it.

"Uh huh!" Donnelle calls, and does a little clap.

Will turns his back to her and bounces his butt in the air as he unzips his pants.

"Turn around! Turn around!" Donnelle cries.

And Will does, just in time to put his hands over his crotch as the pants drop to the floor.

"Oh yeah. Come here, baby."

Will steps out of his pants and straddle-walks up Donnelle's long body.

"Now let's see what's under there." Donnelle peels Will's hands away and runs her own palm up the length of his hardening shaft. She tugs a bit at the underwear waistband, looks up at Will, and slowly licks her lips. "Off," she says.

Talk It Off

The striptease is a way to use anticipation to create fun and excitement in a relationship where you already feel safe and lusty. It works best if you take the time to plan ahead and one of you is ready in provocative and sensual layers. You can even go so far as to use special items of clothing or dreamy fabrics. Think, before you begin, about what kind of music will go best with your presentation of your self.

One way to both avoid undue embarrassment and to double the fun is to do like Will and Donnelle by having your partner act as stage director to your stripper. Decide beforehand how much direction you want and then do your best to meet your partner's demands. To keep the anticipation heightened for both of you, remember to remove clothing gradually, teasingly, one step at a time.

Arrest-Free Public Play

Beth and Joshi live in a small college town. Beth is a professor and Joshi runs the local independent bookstore. Both women are highly respected and easily recognized members to the community. They like to spend their Sundays in the main square. First getting brunch, then browsing the shops, then catching a matinee. Lately, Beth has been lecturing around the country and the two women have had precious little time together. This last Sunday, Joshi had to strain to keep her hands off Beth as they sipped their coffee at their favorite sidewalk café. Students and patrons approached them through much of the meal and Joshi was forced to smile chastely at everyone, while inside she was ready to drag Beth under the wrought-iron table legs. As they watched yet another coed turn to leave, Joshi leaned across the Formica.

"I need to do you so badly it hurts," she said, before straightening up and waving to an approaching store clerk.

Later, in the record shop, Joshi snuck out of the jazz section to purposely squeeze past Beth in the narrow pop aisle.

"Excuse me miss," she whispered hotly in Beth's ear, "but I'll be needing to get under those clothes."

She pressed her pelvis into Beth's soft butt and walked on by.

By the time the two were inside the movie theater, both women were ready to explode. Beth dragged Joshi to the very last aisle on the left, where there was a row of only four seats. She spread her jacket over the third seat and waited for the lights to dim. When the theater went dark, she went right for Joshi's ear.

"Excuse you, you horny thing," she whispered and filled Joshi's ear with her hot breath.

"Jesus," Joshi moaned softly and shot a hand up Beth's thigh. Beth opened her legs for Joshi's hand, reached under her lover's sweater, and closed her fingers tightly around a hardening nipple. When the theater doors brushed open behind them, they momentarily froze in the shaft of lobby light. But once the guy with the tray of popcorn found his seat, they were on each other again, fumbling with zippers, filling each other's mouths with tongue. Beth could feel herself soaking as Joshi worked her clit with her first and second fingers. She tried to hush her shaky breaths and was keenly aware of the danger in crying out if she came. The rows of heads in front of her seemed to swim silently away as her orgasm got closer. "Screw it," she finally thought, and closed her teeth on Joshi's sweater sleeve as the waves crested and crashed through her legs and clenching stomach. When the waves subsided, Beth reached instinctively for Joshi's pants but Joshi stopped her.

"Wait. It'll give us something to do on the way home."

Risk as a Turn-on

The back rows of movie theaters and public trains and buses. Public bathrooms, park trails, and beaches. Airplane lavatories. Darkened alleyways. The guest room at a friend's party. The back or front seats of a publicly parked car. In the midst of slow-moving traffic. These are some of the public places people have confessed to us that they like to get down. Talking hot, kissing, touching, grabbing, even getting each other all the way off in public isn't only hot at the time, but makes for a sexy memory which can serve as a prominent feature in future mental imagery and fantasy. Touching each other in erotic ways in risky places often produces mind-blowing sex. This is because the increased sense of desire overwhelms wisdom or restraint. It works particularly well when paired with the heat that comes out of forced anticipation.

If you don't want to throw down in the town square, be advised that you still have options. You needn't even touch when you are in the midst of other people or in a well-lit public place. Leaning into your partner and letting loose with some hot talk that covers what you want or are going to do to them once you get them out of there, is all it takes to heat up an otherwise routine outing and set the stage for later debauchery.

The Good Sniff

When Justine and Jerome were first together they lived in Georgia. They started to date in late spring, and by the hot summer, the small town where they lived was filled with the strong scents of hibiscus and magnolia and orange blossom. There was an orange tree right outside Justine's apartment window, and as they fell asleep night after passionate night, the scent would seal itself onto their sweating skins. Today, they live in a colder climate, where flowering trees are a rarity, and the smell of sturdy pine is sometimes all the olfactory stimulation they can get.

Soon after Justine's sister sent her a bottle of orange blossom perfume, she and Jerome noticed a heightened level of sexual activity. Jerome felt himself getting physically weak around Justine, and Justine herself was often awash in sexual memories the moment she dabbed the scent on. They mentioned this amazing effect to each other and are now scouring the stores for hibiscus candles and magnolia oils!

Enhancing Your Natural Scent

Besides talking honestly about your natural scents, you can use your sense of smell to enhance sexual pleasure. Exploring should be done as a couple, so that the scents you each use turn both of you on. The more you associate a particular scent with a pleasurable sexual experience together, the more powerful the cue of scent becomes. Remember

Pavlov's dogs? Or Proust? You can have a lot of fun discovering a secret language between the two of you that tells you that more sniffing around might be in the offing later that day or evening.

Take some time to search out different soaps, perfumes, or essential oils, by shopping at body shops, health food stores, and department stores. You can use scent on your body, or you can put fragrance in the air of your room. Just try to be consistent in the fragrances you use. Certain scents are known to inspire feelings of romance and togetherness: ylang ylang, jasmine, bergamot, mandarin, cinnamon, and rose oil. But scent is incredibly personal, so you'll want to see what both of you like.

Scent is a boon to the public communication of private wishes. If you can, find a natural, light-smelling hand cream you both like, with a vegetable or herbal base such as lavender, or almond, or vanilla. That way you can soothe and scent your hands with the cream, and then gently and slowly touch your partner's face, particularly near the nose and mouth. Your message will be received, wordlessly.

Scent tends to be consciously used more by women than by men. Using perfume or scented oils is a great way to send a nonverbal signal that you want to get closer. But it's sexier to take it easy on the amount of scent you use. The key is to put just enough on that your partner simply must get closer to smell it. Because of the heartbeat, fragrance has more resonance on pulse points. Many women tend to put perfume in obvious places: on wrists, behind ears, or on decollete. But when you want to be really seductive, put it somewhere only your partner will smell, like between your thighs, or above your belly button.

When applying scent as a couple, you can add it to the air, a light bulb, or each other's bodies.

Close Sex

Gina is on her side, her right leg up on the pillows, her left curled around the backs of Collin's knees. Collin is kneeling in front of her and deep inside now, his cock thrusting only a quarter of the way out, intense and quick, with his fingers rubbing her clit in fast little circles. He can't get over how well this is going. Gina is watching him now, her face a changing tableau of desire and that ecstatic incomprehension that comes when something new feels so good.

It's amazing for Collin to have Gina look right at him, and to be able to see all of her body like this. So amazing, in fact, that he's having a hard time not coming. But he won't. He looks down at her mound and his disappearing cock and listens hard to her moaning for clues. Is he working her clit right? He is. She's starting to push back, thrusting so hard he has to grab onto her leg with his free hand. He looks again at her face. She's smiling now and shaking her head and he knows she's going to come. He cannot believe how great this is going and why can't it always be like this, and if he only knew that getting close before they did it would make it so . . . oh, god almighty how he loves this woman.

Nonsexual Turn-ons to Bring about Close Sex

For a majority of us, having our partners being present emotionally in a relationship, and being kind and giving and cooperative in whatever work has to go into living together, is some of the hottest foreplay around. The word "foreplay" is deceiving. In actuality, everything we know about sexuality, especially women's sexuality, has shown that there is something crucial before physical foreplay. It is all of the talking and actions that have happened during the last twelve hours or so of togetherness. For many women and some men, being sexually receptive is going to depend a lot on how close she/he feels emotionally to a partner during the last days or week. A hint here: Pulling more than your share of the load task-wise at home can be more sexy than any sexual trick you can pick up in the latest skin mag.

Once those last days have gone well, try some of the turn-ons involved in setting a mood. They may seem mushy, or corny, but things like taking a walk together in the rain, or looking into each other's eyes when you hear a favorite song are very effective ways to build up good feelings. Being verbally close with your partner may seem just plain hard if you are someone who has a difficult time putting emotions into words, but trust us, it is worth trying. Try picking one little episode you have recently shared that makes you love your partner and share it. Sometimes it's difficult to come out and say, "I loved how you were with my family today," or "I loved that look on your face when we got to the top of the trail this morning." But take the risk and utter the tender words.

In this exercise, you will check with each other and see whether you understand what some of your verbal turn-ons might be. As part of the check in, answer the following:

1. How do you think you are doing in the area of acting romantic these days? Rate your score from 0–10.

2. Now ask your partner for her/his rating of your romance quotient on that same scale.

3. What are some of your partner's suggestions for being more romantic?

4. How do you think you are doing in the area of being verbally communicative and emotionally close these days? Rate your own quotient from 0–10.

5. Now ask your partner for her/his assessment.

6. What are some suggestions for being more verbally and emotionally close?

7. How do you think you are doing in the "pulling my share of the weight around here" arena? Rate yourself, 1–10.

8. What does your partner give you as a rating?

9. What are some suggestions for ways in which your partner would like more help with tasks?

Phone Fun

Sarah has finished writing herself a script. She's just watched some hotel porn and it hasn't done the trick. The guy who played the water cooler deliveryman had the same haircut as Marty, which just ended up making her miss him more. If there was ever a time in her life for phone sex, this was it.

Sarah is in New York, three hours ahead of Marty in Seattle, and he still won't be home for another half hour. She looks over her page of phone sex dialogue and decides to do a run-through. There is a full-length gilded mirror to the side of the giant hotel bed and she pulls off her shirt and reclines in front of the glass in her bra.

"Hi love, I've missed you."

Nope, she thinks. Not throaty enough. She tucks her chin to her chest for the next line.

"This enormous four-poster bed they've given me misses you too." ·

That sounded much better.

"I can't stop thinking about that time at the Grand Canyon. Remember? With that cedar bed and the tied sheets?"

Sarah watches herself in the mirror. Her skin is starting to burn.

"You were so good to me that night. I'm coming up with some ideas about how I might be good to you, if you were here."

This last line makes Sarah laugh, and it comforts her to know that Marty will probably laugh with her. She checks the clock, ten minutes to go. Where is that pocket vibrator anyway?

Fabulous Phone Sex

Along with fantasy, it can be fun to make phone sex part of your sex play. It's especially fun to do when you are physically separated from each other for a few days. But many of us are afraid that if we try to vamp it up, we'll burst out laughing. Here are some tips coauthor Aline has heard from the front lines of the male and female professionals who "do it" on the phone.

1. The biggest tip for women is to use a deeper, throatier voice. That, in and of itself, will help you get into the role.

2. Cheat, by writing down a few phrases you want to use, or any words that are so intimidating that you're afraid you'll chicken out of using them. If your partner does some things that you really love, this is the time to suggest that they keep up the good work.

3. Be dramatic. Try to think of yourself in a new role. Pull ideas from characters you have read about, people you have seen in movies or porn videos, or actors and actresses you think are sexy.

4. Or, do the opposite. Instead of drawing your inspiration from fantasyland, think of a wonderful time you and your partner have had together, and tell your partner how exciting it was and how good he or she made you feel.

5. Close your eyes. That way, it's easier to change out of your everyday sense of yourself and let your imagination run wild.

Resources

Sex Stores

Acupressure Institute
1533 Shattuck Avenue
Berkeley, CA 94709
1-800-442-2232
www.acupressure.com
    Series of books and movies that use massage and acupressure to increase sexual pleasure and intimacy.

Blowfish
1-800-325-2569
www.blowfish.com
Online sex source with helpful buying guides organized by sexual preferences.

Eve's Garden
119 West 57th Street, Suite 1201
New York, NY 10019
1-800-848-3837
www.evesgarden.com
Carries movies not widely available as well as books, toys, and games. And despite the name, Eve's has a good selection of movies for men.

Femme Productions
302 Meadowland Drive
Hillsborough, NC 27278
1-800-456-LOVE
www.royalle.com
Candida Royalle's production house carries the full selection of her gently erotic movies.

Good Vibrations   Good Vibrations
1210 Valencia Street   2504 San Pablo Avenue
San Francisco, CA 94130   Berkeley, CA 94702

For general information:
1-800-289-8423
www.goodvibes.com
With "clean, well-lighted" stores in the Bay Area and an enormously popular catalogue and web site, "Good Vibes" has it all. Check out their helpful guide to adult movies, a comprehensive catalog of sex toys, books, and movies for a range of tastes, helpful pamphlets (e.g., *How to Wear a Cock Ring*), and the ever useful chart listing the characteristics of

their dizzying assortment of vibrators. Also has information and products for people with disabilities.

Libida.com

Online sex source for women. Sells toys, books, videos, publishes articles and fiction, and features an anonymous and safe sex chat lounge exclusively for women.

Sinclair Intimacy Institute
P.O. Box 8865
Chapel Hill, NC 27514
1-800-955-0888
www.intimacyinstitute.com
www.bettersex.com

Resources for people over forty and movies on sex and disabilities. Also carries the instructional *Better Sex Videos Series.*

Toys in Babeland   Toys in Babeland
707 E. Pike Street   94 Rivington Street
Seattle, WA 98122   New York, NY 10002

For general information:
1-800-658-9119
www.babeland.com

Friendly, women-owned sex shops with locations in Seattle and New York City. Stocks all kinds of books, movies, and toys, including the Kegelcisor, which is designed to tone the PC muscles of the vagina to enhance orgasm and prevent incontinence.

Xandria Collection
165 Valley Drive
Brisbane, CA 94005
1-800-242-2823
www.xandria.com

Popular provider of books, toys, videos, lingerie/playwear, and accessories. Also carries a special collection of items for people with disabilities, including how-to advice on modifying the use of sex toys.

Online Erotica

www.erotica-readers.com/ERA/index.htm

www.cleansheets.com

www.scarletletters.com

Finding a Sex Therapist

American Association of Sex Educators, Counselors, and Therapists
P.O. Box 5488
Richmond, VA 23220-0488
804-644-3288
www.aasect.org

American Board of Sexology
P.O. Box 1166
Winter Park, FL 32790
www.sexologist.org

Bibliography

Anand, Margo, and Leandra Hussey. 1991. *The Art of Sexual Ecstasy: The Path of Sacred Sexuality for Western Lovers*. New York: J. P. Tarcher.

Berkowitz, Bob. 1998. *His Secret Life: Male Sexual Fantasies* New York: Pocket Books

Blank, Joani, and Ann Whidden. 2000. *Good Vibrations: The New Complete Guide to Vibrators*. San Francisco, Calif.: Down There Press.

Finz, Iris, and Steven Finz. 1999. *Erotic Confessions*. New York: St. Martin's.

———. 1998. *What Turns Us On*. New York: St. Martin's.

Friday, Nancy. 1993. *Forbidden Flowers: More Women's Sexual Fantasies*. New York: Pocket Books.

———. 1998. *My Secret Garden: Women's Sexual Fantasies*. New York: Pocket Books.

Gabriel, Bonnie. 1996. *The Fine Art of Erotic Talk: How to Entice, Excite and Enchant Your Lover with Words*. New York: Bantam Doubleday Dell.

Gach, Michael Reed. 1997. *Acupressure for Lovers: Secrets of Touch for Increasing Intimacy*. New York: Bantam Books.

Gottman, John Mordechai, and Nan Silver. 1999. *The Seven Principles for Making Marriage Work*. New York: Crown Publishing Group.

———. 1994. *Why Marriages Succeed or Fail: What You Can Learn from the Breakthrough Research to Make Your Marriage Last*. New York: Simon & Schuster.

Hite, Shere. 1989. *The Hite Report: A Nationwide Study of Female Sexuality*. New York: Dell Publishing Co.

Love, Dr. Patricia. 1999. *Hot Monogamy: Essential Steps to More Passionate, Intimate Lovemaking*. New York: Plume.

Notarius, Clifford I., and Howard J. Markman. 1994. *We Can Work It Out: How to Solve Conflicts, Save Your Marriage, and Strengthen Your Love for Each Other*. New York: Perigree Publishing.

Vatsyayana, Mallanaga. 1995. *Kama Sutra: An Intimate Photographic Guide to the Arts of Love*. London: Thorsons Publications.

Winks, Cathy, and Semans, Anne. 1997. *The New Good Vibrations Guide to Sex*. San Francisco: Cleis Press.

Aline P. Zoldbrod, Ph.D., is an American Board of Sexology Diplomate, an AASECT certified sex therapist, and a licensed psychologist who for more than thirty years has helped hundreds of men and women learn to communicate their needs and find sexual fulfillment. Author of the award- winning *Sex Smart: How Your Childhood Shaped Your Sexual Life and What to Do About It,* and *Men, Women and Infertility,* she is a frequent contributor to www.sexualhealth.com and www.hisandherhealth.com. Dr. Zoldbrod sees individuals and couples for sex therapy in her private practice in Lexington, Massachusetts, and her model of healthy sexuality can be found on her Web site, www.sexsmart.com.

Lauren Dockett is a professional writer and reviewer. The author of *The Deepest Blue: How Women Face and Overcome Depression* and coauthor of *Facing 30: Women Talk About Constructing a Real Life and Other Scary Rites of Passage,* her erotica and relationship stories have been anthologized in the collections *Uniform Sex* and  *The Moment of Truth.* Ms. Dockett advocates for everyone's right to good sex from her home in the San Francisco Bay Area.

Some Other New Harbinger Titles

The Daughter-In-Law's Survival Guide, Item DSG $12.95

PMDD, Item PMDD $13.95

The Vulvodynia Survival Guide, Item VSG $15.95

Love Tune-Ups, Item LTU $10.95

The Deepest Blue, Item DPSB $13.95

The 50 Best Ways to Simplify Your Life, Item FWSL $11.95

Brave New You, Item BVNY $13.95

Loving Your Teenage Daughter, Item LYTD $14.95

The Hidden Feelings of Motherhood, Item HFM $14.95

The Woman's Book of Sleep, Item WBS $14.95

Pregnancy Stories, Item PS $14.95

The Women's Guide to Total Self-Esteem, Item WGTS $13.95

Thinking Pregnant, Item TKPG $13.95

The Conscious Bride, Item CB $12.95

Juicy Tomatoes, Item JTOM $13.95

Facing 30, Item F30 $12.95

The Money Mystique, Item MYST $13.95

High on Stress, Item HOS $13.95

Perimenopause, 2nd edition, Item PER2 $16.95

The Infertility Survival Guide, Item ISG $16.95

After the Breakup, ATB $13.95

Claiming Your Creative Self, Item CYCS $15.95

Call **toll free, 1-800-748-6273,** or log on to our online bookstore at **www.newharbinger.com** to order. Have your Visa or Mastercard number ready. Or send a check for the titles you want to New Harbinger Publications, Inc., 5674 Shattuck Ave., Oakland, CA 94609. Include $4.50 for the first book and 75¢ for each additional book, to cover shipping and handling. (California residents please include appropriate sales tax.) Allow two to five weeks for delivery.

Prices subject to change without notice.